POSITIVE
SOCIAL WORK
THE ESSENTIAL
TOOLKIT FOR NQSWs

Second Edition

**CRITICAL
SKILLS FOR
SOCIAL WORK**

Other books in this series:

Evidencing CPD: A Guide to Building Your Social Work Portfolio, Second Edition
by Daisy Bogg and Maggie Challis ISBN 978 1 911106 14 2

Personal Safety for Social Workers and Health Professionals
by Brian Atkins ISBN 978 1 909330 33 7

Practice Education in Social Work: Achieving Professional Standards, Second Edition
by Pam Field, Cathie Jasper and Lesley Littler ISBN 978 1 911106 10 4

Active Social Work with Children with Disabilities
by Julie Adams and Diana Leshone ISBN 978 1 910391 94 5

Writing Analytical Assessments in Social Work
by Chris Dyke ISBN 978 1 911106 06 7

Titles are also available in a range of electronic formats. To order please go to our website www.criticalpublishing.com or contact our distributor NBN International, 10 Thornbury Road, Plymouth PL6 7PP, telephone 01752 202301 or email orders@nbninternational.com.

POSITIVE
SOCIAL WORK
THE ESSENTIAL
TOOLKIT FOR NQSWs

Julie Adams and Angie Sheard

Second Edition

CRITICAL
SKILLS FOR
SOCIAL WORK

First published in 2013 by Critical Publishing Ltd
Reprinted in 2014 and 2015
Second edition published in 2017

British Library Cataloguing in Publication Data
A CIP record for this book is available from the British Library

ISBN: 978-1-911106-76-0

This book is also available in the following e-book formats:
MOBI ISBN: 978-1-911106-77-7
EPUB ISBN: 978-1-911106-78-4
Adobe e-book ISBN: 978-1-911106-79-1

Cover design by Out of House
Project Management by Out of House Publishing
Typeset by Newgen Imaging Systems
Printed and bound in Great Britain by TJ International Ltd, Padstow, Cornwall

Critical Publishing
3 Connaught Road
St Albans
AL3 5RX
www.criticalpublishing.com

CONTENTS

Meet the authors

Julie Adams

Julie began working in residential care in 1992, working within children's disability before moving to mainstream settings. Having qualified in 1999, she then moved to field social work and has worked in a variety of settings including child protection, adoption, looking after children and within a hospital setting. Julie worked her way through the ranks from social worker to team manager. Julie mentors social workers, is a Practice Educator and delivers training for students entering social work. Julie has also co-written a second book.

Angie Sheard

Angie began working in residential care with children in 1982 and qualified as a social worker in 1987. After having moved to work in the voluntary sector, she returned to statutory social work in 2002, where she worked predominantly with children, young people and families; she left full-time practice in 2010 to work on other projects and has since worked in advocacy, adult mental health and drug and alcohol education and now combines part-time work with ad hoc project work and training.

Preface

Hello new colleague and welcome to the world of the social worker!

This is an exciting and challenging time for social work with many changes happening all around. Over recent years there has been much negativity both within and around the profession; however, ongoing developments now present us with a good opportunity to move forward positively and embrace the future. We, too, must confess to being sucked into negative ways of thinking ourselves at times but having the opportunity to write this book has been great for us as we have been able to take stock of where things are at for ourselves (you will hear more about taking stock – or 'pressing the pause button' – later on) and for the profession as a whole, and we now find ourselves looking forward to a brighter and more positive and productive future. There are many new developments in social work and we hope that we have managed to give credit to all, and to get things right too, in our work here. We also acknowledge the hard work of colleagues in the development of the service and recognise that we are part way down the path to a new future, and that this continues to be strewn with challenges.

This is a great time to qualify as a social worker and this book is written for all Newly Qualified Social Workers (NQSWs) wherever you live or practise. Though we discuss developments in England, this book applies equally to all NQSWs in the UK who are about to enter the profession and who will be looking to thrive in their first year of practice.

Things are happening fast and you are a part of it! This book is designed to help you along the way – throughout your Assessed and Supported Year in Employment (ASYE) and beyond. For existing workers in England who are directly affected by new developments, there may be uncertainty and this in itself may lead to some experienced workers becoming uncertain in the short term and thinking that too much is happening too quickly. The advantage for you is that this is all new to you as an NQSW and you will be in it from the beginning with no preconceived ideas or expectations of 'how it used to be'.

The book introduces a Toolkit which will assist in gathering evidence for the ASYE (for those of you in England) and each chapter is designed to link to the Professional Capabilities Framework (PCF). Once you have worked through the chapters you will be encouraged to think about which areas of capability you are developing, to fill in the Toolkit and to build up your evidence portfolio. The earlier you begin this process the better, and the Toolkit is designed to be used as a prompt and a talking point in supervision. If you do not need or want to use the Toolkit then the chapters stand alone and will be of great benefit to you all.

The chapters in this book will help you to gain a greater understanding about yourself and how you deal with stress and difficult situations, help you achieve a positive work–life balance, develop your emotional resilience, show you where to look for support and what to watch out for along the way; in short – how to be the best you can be. Each chapter contains a case study and activities designed to make you think about your practice. At the end of each chapter you will be given ideas on where to look for further information and support and you will be encouraged to think about what new habits you will develop from your learning. There is a wealth of public information on the internet, and many good publications which cover the topics in this book; your colleagues, family and friends are all there to assist too.

This is not a theoretical book – although some theory is referenced – rather, it is written as a practical, down-to-earth guide which aims to help all NQSWs as they move into practice. Though specifically targeted at NQSWs, this book is also written with students, practice educators, tutors, managers and university colleagues in mind. All of you will find this book useful and the chapter which looks at how assessors and supervisors can utilise the Toolkit will be of particular interest to anyone who is assessing during the ASYE; Practice Educators may also find the Toolkit invaluable when working with students who are being introduced to the PCF.

All that is left for us to do is to wish you good luck and a long, successful and rewarding career.

Best regards
Julie and Angie

Acknowledgements

In writing this book, we would like to acknowledge the following:

Our colleagues, friends and families, who have listened and encouraged us, but most especially Darren and Mike, who showed great patience – and cooked our tea – while we were writing this book.

Karen Gilbank and Kerry Welch, NQSWs, for their review of the first chapter and words of encouragement.

Our newly qualified colleagues who are just starting out on their journey, and who have worked hard to get this far and who will take the profession forward.

All social workers who continue to work extremely hard under often challenging conditions, to protect and support the most vulnerable in our communities, and of course, the many people who use social care services, and who face daily difficulties, the likes of which most of us can only imagine.

Last, but by no means least, our four-legged friends who 'helped' along the way. Sadly, during the writing of this book both Mollie and Bobs passed away, but Henry continues to make his presence known quite loudly.

1   Introduction to your Toolkit

Welcome to the first chapter in the book which will help you along the way during your first year in practice. By now you will have probably completed or be reaching the end of your social work course and should be looking forward to your first year working as a registered and qualified social worker. How are you feeling? Excited? Scared? Or a bit of both? Great – and lucky you! Well done and congratulations on your success so far.

In this chapter we introduce our Toolkit and discuss what it is and how it has evolved, why you may need it and how you can use it to your advantage as you start on your new career. Readers in England will be undertaking their first year in practice assessed under the new Assessed and Supported Year in Employment (ASYE) requirements and the Toolkit will help collate your evidence for this. Those of you who may not be obliged to fulfil the requirements of the ASYE may still find the Toolkit useful in helping you to reflect on practice. The Toolkit forms only one part of the book – the chapters themselves are designed to support you with or without the Toolkit and will be greatly beneficial to all. Remember too that our Toolkit is one of many tools that have been developed to help you as you begin in practice and by no means do we claim it to be the best, but rather another option which some may choose to make use of.

Years of study, learning, placements and assignments are behind you and you are about to enter a new world, one in which you will be expected to practise to the highest standards of capability and to uphold the ethics and values of the profession. As we have already mentioned, things continue to change rapidly in social work and one of the most important areas where this can be seen is in the changes to the way in which NQSWs enter the workplace. The ASYE was one of the many recommendations made by the Social Work Task Force following their work which looked at the profession and how things might be improved and developed. This book is designed to help you to get the best out of your initial year as a social worker; it will provide you with a level of confidence and a firm foundation as you progress and develop within the profession.

The ASYE is part of a much wider range of developments within the social work profession and as such should not be viewed in isolation. In addition to the links we make here, it should also be viewed in the context of many ongoing developments within the profession including changes to both the standards for supervision (ie, the Standards for Employers and Supervision Framework) and continuing professional development (CPD), the introduction of the Knowledge and Skills statements and the proposals for increasing the effectiveness of working with other agencies, both voluntary and statutory. It is well worth reading up on what is happening in all of these areas as you may well be directly affected by these developments.

WHAT IS THE TOOLKIT?

(Please note – though we will discuss the Toolkit now, you will find it at the back of the book and it is also available to download from the Critical Publishing website www.criticalpublishing. com/asset/126677/1/Positive_Social_Work_Toolkit.pdf.) A short example is included below.

The Toolkit is a simple but very practical tool to help you as you work through your first year in practice. In essence it is a document that is designed to help you to collate some of the evidence for your portfolio and we encourage you to develop this as you go along. It is a working document and you will see as you read through the book that we talk about developing good habits, and continuing the ones that you learned throughout your journey through university. Developing the Toolkit is the first good habit that we suggest you get into, and as soon as you possibly can.

Have a look at the Toolkit. It is quite a big document with lots of questions on it but please don't be put off by that. You are not expected to answer all of these questions – you may choose not to answer any! The questions are there simply to encourage you to reflect on practice. We all get stuck at times and the aim of the exercise is to support you when this happens. If you are in the habit of gathering evidence for your assessment as you go along, then you may not need to use the questions as much – they are a prompt.

As you will no doubt be aware, during your ASYE your professional capability will be assessed through the Professional Capabilities Framework (PCF), which is the overarching standards framework, applicable to all social workers. (You will also have to meet the specific role requirements set out in the Knowledge and Skills statements, for whichever area of work you choose to enter.) As you study the Toolkit you will see that it contains nine sections, which correspond to the nine sections of the PCF – you may hear this referred to as 'the fan' or 'the rainbow'. You will be familiar with the PCF and you will know that there are different levels of competence which need to be demonstrated and which relate to your level of experience. The Toolkit relates directly to the PCF levels for NQSWs who are working through the ASYE.

As you will see in the Toolkit, for each area of professional capability in the fan (eg professionalism, diversity) there are five distinct sections.

- The first relates to the corresponding PCF domain.

- The second gives a general statement regarding the area of practice covered in the section.

- The third gives you an idea of where you may find this book useful in supporting your evidence base, though many issues will overlap across the domains.

- The fourth is a series of statements and questions – the purpose of this section is to make you think and to allow for critical reflection. This should prompt you to recall incidents or events which you can then use to evidence your development. Remember that these are only prompts but they do address the areas in which you will need to develop capability throughout the year. Answering these questions alone will not guarantee you success – this is one part of your journey.

- The last section is the most important for you and this is where you are invited to fill in notes and examples of your practice. Together with the other evidence you will have collected, this will build into the portfolio which forms part of the work that is required for your assessment.

EXAMPLE TOOLKIT

PCF 5 – Knowledge

Overview: The knowledge you have developed in different areas including the law, policy and procedure, human development and the influences upon this. Different social work models and theories, and how you use this knowledge in practice.

Predominant links to Chapters 4, 5, 6, 7, 9

- o Describe your knowledge base. What knowledge do you need to do your job effectively and where does this come from, how have you used the knowledge gained throughout your time at university to your and the service users' best advantage, do you feel that this effectively equipped you for your role, what areas of knowledge do you use daily, weekly or less often, which specialist areas of knowledge do you use in your current role?

- o Which areas of theoretical knowledge do you currently use and how, how have you developed this in practice, what further reading or research have you completed in this area, which areas do you find particularly difficult or challenging, how have you addressed this, are there any theories that you particularly use and apply methodically or habitually, or are there some that you don't – why not? Are you heavily reliant on a few theoretical models, which ones and why? Do you test out different theories, why do you do this?

- o What are the most significant policies and procedures that your practice is guided by, how familiar are you with these, how do they shape your work, do you feel that you understand them all fully?

- o What legislation does your service work under, how does this impact upon your role as a social worker, which pieces of legislation do you use the most, which pose the most challenge, how do you implement the legislation with service users and ensure their understanding and compliance, what action do you take when legal agreements are breached?

- o What social work models do you use when working with service users, are there some that you find work better than others, others that you have yet to try, or some that you find do not work for you – why?

○ What new knowledge have you acquired since you qualified, how did this come about and why, how are you using this in your practice, where has this learning come from, what have you learned from reading, supervision, colleagues, service users or others, what do you feel has been your most valuable lesson and why, how do you keep up to date with new developments in social work, what articles, journals, books or magazine articles have you read?

○ Where do you go when you do not know the answer, what happens when you are faced with a situation or question that you do not have an answer for, how do you use others' experience and knowledge to further your own and to benefit the service user, have you identified any gaps in your knowledge in terms of theory, policy and procedure, legislation, what have you done to address this?

○ Use this space to add your own examples, evidence, plans, reflection.

BACKGROUND TO THE TOOLKIT

You might be thinking – what is this 'Toolkit'? Where did it come from? How did it come into being? How was it developed? One thing is certain: it looks and feels very different from our original idea when we were asked to write this book. The idea for the book came about following training that we developed which addressed the issues of stress and burnout for social workers. The training originally included sessions on work–life balance, time management, stress versus burnout, taking work home and many other issues which caused concern for those already working in the profession. Throughout the session the participants were encouraged to complete what at the time was called 'My Personal Survival Kit'. This was then taken away to be developed by the individuals into a resource which would enable them to care for themselves in a more positive way.

Course members began by thinking back to why they wanted to be a social worker initially and to what gets them up in the morning. You will see that we have kept that question in the Toolkit in its current form, as we feel that this is a good way to get back to basics, and to keep us grounded. Following this initial question, the group went to fill in sections about how they managed stress, and how they would develop their own support network. They also identified their own strengths and vulnerabilities and planned what they were going to do to address some of the issues that the course raised for them. This course was well received and we gained some excellent feedback from it. Many of these elements are included in the book as you see it today.

However, as times have moved on and the changes and improvements in social work have now begun to be implemented, the focus of our work has changed. Following discussions with peers and feedback from other professionals we reflected (as all good social workers do!) and recognised that we needed to change the focus of our work to be more in line with current positive changes in the profession. We felt that we had been guilty at times of being caught in the culture of cynicism and negativity around social work and wanted to change this for ourselves, for others but mostly for you, the NQSW who is just starting on what will hopefully be a long and rewarding career path.

Together with this change in focus, the development of the ASYE and the PCF and the change in regulatory body, we felt that a more positive approach to the Toolkit was required and so out went the concept of 'surviving' and in came 'thriving'.

HOW YOU CAN GET THE BEST FROM YOUR TOOLKIT

Our suggested way for using the Toolkit would be as follows but this is only one example; this is for *you* and the most important thing is for you to make this tool work for *you*. What works for one may not work for another.

- Have a read through the book and familiarise yourself with the Toolkit.

- Either download the Toolkit from www.criticalpublishing.com or make up your own Word document – you don't need to type in all of the questions. Either way ensure that you have a paper copy which is your working document – you can add to this easily wherever you are.

- Additionally you might want to set up a folder on your computer to store evidence and/or have a paper folder to put things in.

- Discuss how you will use the Toolkit with your manager/assessor as soon as possible and let them have a copy. You might want to include it in your learning agreement (this will be negotiated between your manager/assessor and yourself when you begin your ASYE and is similar to the learning agreement you had while on placement).

- Have the Toolkit as a standing agenda item in your supervision sessions.

- As soon as you can, start to collect your evidence.

- Set aside a regular (short) time each week to jot down your thoughts on the working document.

- Set aside a longer time each month to review where you are at (this may be your supervision time) and to then type up your Toolkit fully.

- Refer back to the book regularly as you go along.

You will be surprised at how quickly your evidence builds and you will be also on top of any areas where you need to improve things.

A word about the Toolkit, the PCF and the HCPC standards of proficiency

In August 2012 the Health and Care Professions Council (HCPC) assumed responsibility for the registration of social workers in England. As a part of this process the HCPC developed standards of proficiency for all social workers. Social workers in Scotland, Northern Ireland and Wales have their own registration and regulatory bodies (please see below for details) and they have also agreed a memorandum of understanding (MOU), which allows for mutual collaboration between the HCPC and themselves.

The PCF and the HCPC standards are similar in many areas but have different functions. The HCPC standards provide a baseline for all social workers in England; this is what you need to know and understand as you enter the profession and this will allow you to become a registered social worker. The PCF provides a framework for social workers in their developing career and outlines the capabilities that we all need to reach as we progress from NQSW stage through to Principal Social Worker (should you choose to).

As we have already seen, the Toolkit is linked directly to the PCF, and as we now know this is similar in many areas to the HCPC standards. Because this book is aimed at supporting the ASYE our focus is solely on the PCF and enabling you to gather evidence for this. For this reason you will only see elements of the PCF addressed in the Toolkit. However, it is worth noting that the PCF and the HCPC standards do overlap and this has been mapped by the (now defunct) College of Social Work in a very useful document which can be found on the internet (see link below in 'Taking it further'). It is also worth noting here that though originally developed by the College of Social Work, responsibility

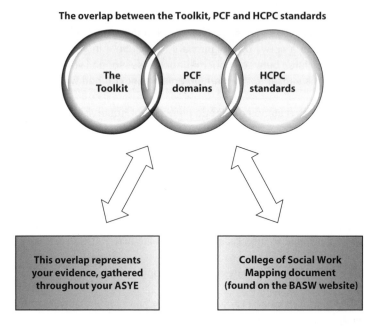

The overlap between the Toolkit, PCF and HCPC standards

The Toolkit

PCF domains

HCPC standards

This overlap represents your evidence, gathered throughout your ASYE

College of Social Work Mapping document (found on the BASW website)

for the PCF now lies with BASW. During the period of transition, a review of the PCF was carried out and this recommended some updates to PCF 9 – work that is currently underway and will be published in due course.

It can be useful to view the overlap as in the figure on the previous page.

We hope that this introduction has made the purpose of the Toolkit clear and that you are now raring to get on with it.

All that is left for us to do is to send you our very best wishes for your ASYE and for a long and fulfilling career.

Now, it's over to you …

TAKING IT FURTHER

Bogg, D, Challis, M (2016) Evidencing CPD: A Guide to Building Your Social Work Portfolio. Northwich: Critical Publishing

Colleagues in England:

www.basw.co.uk/PCF

www.hcpc-uk.org

www.skillsforcare.org.uk/socialwork

Colleagues in other parts of the UK:

Scottish Social Services Council: www.sssc.com

Care Council for Wales: www.ccwales.org.uk

Northern Ireland Social Care Council: www.niscc.info

2 What to expect as you enter practice

INTRODUCTION

This chapter will help you as you take your first steps into your social work career. We will cover getting advice, preparing for and landing your ideal job in social work (including completing the application form, and some mock interview questions) and how to prepare for your first day, week and months in practice. This will help you to assert yourself, to be aware of office politics and culture and will encourage you to remember what you have been taught so you continue to develop good habits. Reference to your ASYE will also be made.

- o Knowing what you want
- o Preparation
- o The interview
- o Your first day, week and coming months
- o Your first supervision
- o Asserting yourself
- o Team dynamics
- o Developing good habits

Links to:

PCF 1 – Professionalism

PCF 5 – Knowledge

PCF 8 – Contexts and Organisations

PCF 9 – Professional Leadership

KNOWING WHAT YOU WANT

Social work is diverse and there are many career paths you can travel. One thing is for certain, you'll never get bored, and each area is full of its own challenges and opportunities, whether in the voluntary, public or private sector. However, we strongly advise you to think carefully about the direction you want to go in and focus on this area. All your skills will be transferable but you need a good foundation to start with. You will also need stability during your ASYE.

Keep an open mind, but knowing where you want to end up will be beneficial as you start to look for your first job as a qualified social worker. It will help you keep focused with your research. It is important here to also think about the current climate and the difficulties that some NQSWs are facing in getting their ideal role – see our section on this subject in Chapter 10.

Once you've decided where you want to work, go online and do your research. There are lots of websites that offer you help and advice (see Chapter 9) but a particularly good source is www.communitycare.co.uk, which offers details of a variety of jobs available throughout the UK and further afield, live debates and updates of practice issues. You can also sign up for job alerts. There are other places too such as job fairs and recruitment agencies and your local and national newspapers, most of which are now available online too.

When setting off in search of your ideal social work job, it's great to have clear expectations of what you want and know what your employer will want from you. However, be aware of what an 'expectation' is and what 'reality' is. Here are two examples of what can happen when details aren't checked carefully.

YOUR APPLICATION FORM

Most application forms are now completed online. You can save it and return to it as you fill it in before finally submitting it. Here are a few points to remember, but look online too as there's lots of information out there to help you do the perfect application, for example at www.totaljobs.com.

- Allow yourself plenty of time to complete the form and don't try to do it all at once.
- Read the job specification and essential and desirable criteria, ensuring you show how you meet these categories.
- Give examples of your experience – include any voluntary or placement work – it is not enough to say that you can do it – you must give specific examples for each criterion; for example: *when I was on placement I completed about 20 assessments with young/older people and from this I developed a plan of work.*
- Once you have completed the application form go back and ensure that you have covered each one of the requirements of the person specification.
- Declare any convictions or cautions – this doesn't mean you won't get the job.
- Include referees but do get their permission first.

Case Study – Great expectations

Mollie arrived for her first day in her new job as an NQSW. She was shown into the office to a clear desk near the window. Mollie thought this was great; she had a good position in the office and the desk was free of clutter and ready for her to 'make her own'. Mollie had brought a few personal items such as her favourite mug and a photo of friends and family, which she set out on the desk. Having her own desk made Mollie feel comfortable and secure and already part of the team. Shortly after setting up her desk, Mollie was then taken to another department to have her photograph taken for her new ID badge. On her return, Mollie was shocked to find that her personal items had been taken off her desk and placed into a box, and another social worker was sitting at the desk, and was using the phone and the computer. Her manager explained to Mollie that some social workers no longer had the luxury of having their own desk and that 'agile working' and 'hot desking' had been introduced some time ago. All desks therefore had to be free of clutter and personal items so that any social worker that needed to could use them. Mollie was very upset; she had not understood what 'hot desking and agile working' had meant when she saw it on the job description.

Bob has recently started his first job as a supervising social worker in an independent fostering agency. When Bob saw the advertisement, he thought he had found the perfect job. The advert talked about the benefits of 'working from home', offering support via online supervision and fortnightly team meetings with colleagues at a mutual venue and flexible working hours. Bob thought this sounded great – no getting up at the crack of dawn, no rush hour traffic and no boss watching his every move. However, after a few months in the job, Bob found that the reality of these 'benefits' was that he had a distinct lack of contact with colleagues and limited support networks. He was also developing bad habits, becoming isolated and lonely, and had a lack of positive role models to help influence his learning and good practice. Bob also needed to be observed by his supervisor/practice educator as he made his journey along his ASYE, which was proving very difficult. As an NQSW, Bob no longer thought that the benefits appeared so attractive.

Both Mollie and Bob have been 'disillusioned' as a result of their own lack of understanding. These are the types of things that you may want to ask about at interview so that you are clear about what is an expectation and what is truth. It is better than having shattered illusions and blaming the job for your false expectations. Be clear at the beginning about what is being offered and ensure that the job is the right one for you.

Some organisations will allow a curriculum vitae (CV), although most usually only want an application form. There is information available about setting up your CV at websites such as https://cvwriting.net.

PREPARATION

Think about the knowledge and skills you have acquired while achieving your degree (and before too). Think about the challenges you have already overcome and how proud you are of what you have achieved to date. Remember it is about what you *have* done and not talking about what you have not done – think about your achievements and translate them into *experience.*

When you have been successful with your application form you will be invited to interview. The key to a good interview is preparation. Good preparation is never wasted and, if you don't get the first job you apply for, it will be valuable for the next interview. Remember all you have learned about 'feedback' and 'reflective practice'. Reflect upon the advice given in your feedback and learn from your experience, putting this new learning into your next interview. You need to understand the role and tasks of the social worker within the team you are applying for. You can often visit the team prior to interview but if not, there is often a telephone number of a contact person on the advertisement for you to ring for further information. Do some research on the organisation. Look online at their website, read their 'mission statement', 'vision' or 'plan' which outlines the organisation's wider aims and objectives.

Prior to interview, you may be given details of a presentation to prepare and bring to interview, or you may be informed that you will have to do a test on the day, which may be a written exercise or an 'in tray' exercise (a list of activities/jobs that you would have to complete in a day's work; you have to prioritise the list, deciding on those that require immediate action and those you can leave until later). Don't be put off as this is a normal expectation for most social work interviews. Ensure you understand the question that is being asked and if in doubt – ask. Keep it simple but don't get too stressed, it is only part of the process.

If you have to do a presentation:

- don't overload your PowerPoint/presentation slides;
- practise your timings – don't speak too fast;
- if possible practise and get feedback from an audience;
- speak clearly and give eye contact;
- don't put things in that you don't understand.

ACTIVITY · PLANNING FOR AN INTERVIEW

Prior to interview:

Think about, and make a list of, your knowledge and skills –
what you learned on placement and/or during any other types of
employment you have had to date including any voluntary work.

Think about how you can transfer these skills to best meet the requirements
of the job you are applying for. Think about how you link social work theories
to practice and utilise your emotional intelligence (see Chapter 5).

Think about what questions you may be asked at interview and scenarios you
can give that demonstrate your experience and knowledge, giving examples.

Make a list of your key strengths and the qualities that you will bring to
any team. Also consider areas for development so that you are aware
of this when the interviewers ask you about any training needs.

Think about any questions you may want to ask the panel as you will
be given the opportunity towards the end of the interview. Remember
this is a two-way process: you are finding out about them and what they
can offer you as well as the other way around. This is your chance to
clarify anything you want to know about the job and working conditions,
etc. It shows you have given serious consideration to the job.

What should I wear?

There are no hard and fast rules about what to wear for your interview. These days there
is a lot of competition for jobs and therefore we would advise you to present yourself in
the best way you can. Look clean and smart and well laundered. Be yourself but ensure
you are comfortable so that you are able to concentrate throughout the interview rather
than worrying about what you are wearing.

THE INTERVIEW

Your interview will often be undertaken with a panel of three people. The panel may
consist of another social worker, team manager, a senior manager or perhaps someone
from another organisation. All interviews are different and different jobs require different
skills and experience so we cannot give you a definitive list of the questions you will be
asked. You may be given different scenarios to get you to think and show your experience
and demonstrate your knowledge. The scenarios may be linked to your chosen area of
work and will not be intended to trip you up. They are a good opportunity for you to demonstrate your thinking skills even if you have not had direct experience of the particular
situation.

ACTIVITY · A MOCK INTERVIEW

Presentation: Prepare a five-minute presentation on your understanding of equal opportunities and anti-discriminatory practice and how you use this within your practice.

Example questions:

What personal attributes and qualities would you bring to the team?

Why did you want a career in social work?

What is your understanding of confidentiality?

What skills and relevant experience do you have for the post?

What are your key strengths and areas for development?

How do you deal with stress and what are your coping strategies?

How do you manage conflict?

What is your understanding and expectations of supervision?

What is your understanding of your Assessed and Supported Year in Employment?

(You will be given some specific questions about your particular job.)

Scenarios:

A member of your team has been making you feel uncomfortable while you are at work. They have been saying that you are doing everything wrong and that you will never be a good social worker. What would you do?

You are working with a service user who has taken a shine to you. They ask you out on a date. What would you do?

Obviously, these are only examples of *some* of the types of things you may be asked. Your interview will be geared to your particular job and the level of job you are applying for – NQSW and not Senior Social Worker. These questions are intended just to get you thinking about your interview. Your interviewers will not be expecting you to be able to answer every question in depth as they understand your nerves and your limited experience at this stage in your career.

During the interview, think about your answers and ask if you need any questions repeating or clarifying. Remember – active listening skills. Be aware of your body language but make sure you remember to smile. Don't fidget or talk over panel members. Be polite and be positive. Towards the end of the interview you will usually be given the opportunity to ask any questions that you may have about the job and the conditions of employment.

After the interview, don't worry about it. It's over and you can't change it now. Hopefully, you'll soon receive that all important call saying you've got the job – and well done! However, if you are not successful, don't be disillusioned. Make sure you ask for feedback, but wait a few days before you do, so that you are calm and can take in what you are being told. You will learn from the experience and you can put all you've learned into your next interview. Keep up the good work and you'll soon find that perfect job.

YOUR FIRST DAY, WEEK AND COMING MONTHS

You are bound to have some nerves and you may doubt yourself and your knowledge and experience as you make the transition from the learning environment of university and being on placement, to a fully fledged employee. This is normal. Talk to the other NQSWs who were on your course and ask about how they are feeling or what they have experienced so far. We've all been there and other social workers will help you through this important period in your career.

On your first day, it is likely that you will be taken through all the basics such as:

* introductions to the team;
* tea and coffee/toilets;
* hours of work;
* how you are paid and pensions;
* health and safety and fire procedures;
* how the team works – signing in and out;
* duty and caseloads;
* arranging ID badges and parking permits;
* computer log-in details and email access;
* access to computer training;
* laptop/mobile telephone.

Your manager should talk to you about your induction. You'll probably feel tired at the end of your first week with the overload of information you've been given and the new experience but, again, this is normal. Don't make judgements about things too quickly and allow yourself time to settle in first.

ACTIVITY · REMEMBERING WHAT YOU'VE BEEN TAUGHT

Just before you start your new job, think back … it was not so long ago that you undertook two work-based placements and you were meeting deadlines for your placement and for completing your degree.

What did you really learn from these placements?
List five positive outcomes from each one.

Don't dwell on any negatives but consider what you wish you had done differently and, importantly, why?

How did your practice improve from these experiences?

How did you use the support that was in place? How did you survive?

What is different now and why?

How can you ensure any new fears are overcome?

You will have used a 'reflective journal' throughout your training. Read through your journal to remind you about your experiences and importantly to help you overcome some of your fears. You may want to continue this journal during your first few months to help you continue with your reflective learning and to help you think about your transition into your new role.

Take stock and think about all these things. Remember: You've already come a long way and you deserve to be where you are today. Be POSITIVE.

Inductions vary within different organisations. However, all NQSWs, regardless of setting and organisation, should have an in-depth induction linked to their ASYE. A good induction is important as it allows you to quickly learn about the expectations upon you as an NQSW, and how to perform in your job more effectively and build your confidence.

Think about what you want from your induction and how you can get the best from this experience. Write down a list of questions you may want answers to, things you want to know and places you may want to visit as part of your induction. Ask your manager as you think of different things as you go along. Your manager may link you up with an experienced practitioner(s) for the first few weeks and arrange for you to shadow them in their practice. Make notes along the way and make a list of useful contacts as you meet them. Make the most of your induction and get out and about visiting partner agencies and finding out about all you can, while you have the time to do this. Make links and build your support networks.

PRACTICALITIES

As you are settling in and during your induction you will no doubt need answers to some practicalities in order to do your job more effectively. Here are a few things you may need to consider or find out about.

- What administration support do you have?
- How do you gain access to the building if you are working early or late?
- Is there a list of useful phone numbers?
- Do we use dirty or clean mail (handwritten or typed envelopes)?
- Who is responsible for booking rooms or meetings?
- Where are meetings held?
- Does the team have access to any resources?
- Who does the team deal with most (other professionals)?
- When are team meetings held?
- Is there a script for answering the phone?
- Where are the best parking spaces?
- Where's the nearest sandwich shop?
- What are the kitchen/fridge rules? (Yes, they really exist!)

YOUR FIRST SUPERVISION

During your first supervision session with your supervisor and/or manager they should help ensure that you are 'finding your feet' and that you are settling into the team. They should be checking that your induction is working well and that you are not feeling too overwhelmed. All social workers have supervision; however, during their ASYE all NQSWs should receive weekly supervision for the first six weeks, then fortnightly for the duration of the first six months and at least monthly thereafter. As an NQSW you should also have a protected caseload, particularly during your ASYE. You should have protected time for personal development, which normally equates to 10 per cent over the course of the year (see Chapter 9). Your ongoing supervision will become more structured as you get more cases allocated to you. Use supervision to clarify:

- your roles and responsibilities;
- organisational structures and goals;
- policies and procedures;
- reflection;
- the local community – resources;
- caseloads.

Case Study – Getting started in a new job

Alex has been in his first job for six weeks. He has completed his initial induction and feels settled and well orientated as he starts along his ASYE. He has been allocated ten cases and already feels prepared and is looking forward to 'getting started'. Alex asked for supervision with his manager on the fifth week of his induction and has already got his next four supervision dates booked into his diary. Alex has contacted each of his families and made appointments to meet them to discuss the care plan that is in place for each service user, so that he can become more familiar with the care planning process and case management responsibilities. The reason Alex feels confident is that he has prepared well and has used his induction and his team appropriately.

Alex found out which cases he would be allocated prior to allocation; he read background information on each case using the electronic files; he made contact with other professionals involved on each case for initial discussions; asked appropriate questions about the organisation; clarified roles and responsibilities of his own job and that of others; visited other departments and took advantage of shadowing his colleagues/peers throughout his induction. Alex asked the appropriate questions and considered what he had already learned during his placements and how this could prepare him for his first social work job.

Alex has made an excellent start. He has taken time for preparation and getting the most from his induction and his colleagues and, importantly, using his supervisor to get what he needed, for example, by asking for information about cases he would be allocated so he could research them first. Think about what Alex has done and how you can learn from his approach.

ASSERTING YOURSELF

There is little doubt that you will be given cases fairly soon into your first few weeks. It is best to get into doing the job and settling in and being part of the team. Remember what you've learned. You have experienced what it's like being a social worker, you've proved you can do the job; after all you've got your degree and you passed the interview. Ask if you are unsure as it is better to clarify things at the beginning. Don't be afraid of asking those silly questions – they're usually not as silly as you think. Be open to new work experiences and alternative perspectives from others. Your motivation will help your manager to build upon your skills and knowledge base. Think about how you can take on additional responsibilities as you progress – but keep control and stay safe. Do additional reading to help you with your cases and new subject areas to help build your knowledge as you develop. Balance knowledge with practical application.

If you are an NQSW who was a 'work-based student' and have previously been employed as an unqualified worker within your team, being assertive is particularly important. Remember, you have a great knowledge of the team, but you are now a qualified social worker and you need to be given the same opportunity as any other NQSWs. This does not mean that you should be allocated lots of complex cases and be expected to manage them, just because you have some prior knowledge of the team. You are now in a different role. Discuss this early on with your manager/supervisor if you have any worries or concerns about this.

OFFICE CULTURE

Take a little time to see what goes on within the office – how people act and get on together. You'll soon know what is and is not acceptable. Listen to how people answer the phone. Is there a certain 'speech' you have to give or are there certain answers to certain questions that you have to give? How does 'duty' work and are you expected to do a certain number of days on duty? Are there certain expectations within the team, any 'unwritten rules'? Is there a tea fund? It is perhaps best not to talk about your political or religious persuasion or any sensitive subjects, at least until you feel safe and comfortable within your organisation and know your colleagues. You will notice that some colleagues seem to do different hours and many offices work a flexitime system. You will find what suits you as the time passes. If you are a smoker then you will learn early on where the smokers congregate and how this all works. Some colleagues will socialise outside work and some will not. It may take a while to work all of this out, but you will and soon you will stop feeling like the 'newbie'. One thing worth mentioning here is that if you find this difficult to manage and it takes you a while to settle, just imagine if you were to work as an agency social worker in which case you would have to face this quite often. Though – take it from us – it does get easier!

TEAM DYNAMICS

Your team is important to you and your journey along your ASYE. It should be a key asset to your continual progress and development. You are now an important member of your team, and your role within the team is vital.

Think about your position within the team. Not only are you 'the new person' but you may also feel that your age will influence how you fit in. Are you a mature person with lots of previous experience or a younger person with limited life experience, and how may this impact upon you and your colleagues? Think about friendships you may make with colleagues and the different personalities within the team and who is on your 'wavelength'.

Team meetings are a good opportunity for you to look at how your team functions and pulls together and how relationships within the team are formed. You should have regular team meetings, which will be multifunctional. They will allow the manager to disseminate information from senior managers, enable the team to discuss cases, make decisions and support one another, and act as a learning environment to support everyone's practice. Think about the strengths within your team and the structure of the team and/or any weaknesses within the team and why they are weaknesses. Think about how to get the most from your team. Think about the positive relationships within the team and any that you may want to avoid, and again why. Good collaborative team working will improve morale and job satisfaction within the team and throughout the organisation and thus improve the lives of service users.

DEVELOPING GOOD HABITS

Try and develop good habits from the start and remember all you have learned so far. Throughout this book we will encourage you to prepare and develop good habits. Remember:

* Learn to prioritise your work.
* Develop good organisational skills.
* Plan your work.
* Always take your lunch break – try to have at least half an hour every day.
* Try to leave on time.
* Don't be afraid to ask for help.
* Take your time off in lieu (TOIL) if you do build it up.
* Turn off your work phone when you are not at work.
* Have a healthy work–life balance.
* Recognise stress and anxiety and take necessary action.
* Create support networks.
* Get the most from your supervision.
* Don't try to run before you can walk.
* Reflective practice – consider using your reflective journal.

Your new habits

Think about how you can make your transition into practice seamless and what new habits you can put in place. Have a look at the list above and note down those things that you will do as a result of your learning.

Your Toolkit – Consider the first few months in your new job. How will you prepare yourself for this transition from student to NQSW and how will you prepare yourself to get the most from your ASYE? Think about possible scenarios and good examples of your practice, linking your theory to practice. Are you professionally assertive? Are you making the most of your supervision? Reflect on the chapter and start to think about any evidence that you can include from this for your assessment.

TAKING IT FURTHER

Sidell, N, Smiley, D (2008) Professional Communication Skills in Social Work. Allyn & Bacon, Longman

Websites:

https://cvwriting.net

www.mindtools.com/pages/article/professionalism.htm

www.totaljobs.com/careers-advice/cvs-and-applications/application-form-questions-one

3 Maximising your professional capabilities

INTRODUCTION

This chapter will help you think about your values and ethics and the importance of giving consideration to how your own upbringing may impact upon your role as a social worker and upon the decisions you make. It will allow you to think about your professional image, relationships with colleagues and service users and keeping appropriate boundaries in place. We also discuss the need to ask for feedback, challenge other people's views and opinions or the way in which they practise, and how we ourselves sometimes need to change. There are case studies and activities to help you consider ethical and moral dilemmas and boundaries.

- o   Professionalism
- o   Your professional image
- o   Professional relationships
- o   Social media networks
- o   Boundaries
- o   Values and ethics
- o   Moral and ethical dilemmas
- o   Feedback
- o   Changing ourselves and challenging others

Links to:

PCF 1 – Professionalism

PCF 2 – Values and Ethics

PCF 7 – Intervention and Skills

PCF 8 – Contexts and Organisations

PROFESSIONALISM

Social work has come a long way with regard to developing its professionalism and the protection of the title 'Social Worker' by law was an important step forward. Anyone using this title must be registered with the HCPC or they may be subject to prosecution and a fine of up to £5,000. The HCPC's PCF and the Standards of Proficiency (SoP) have enhanced the reputation of the profession further.

Guidance states that 'professionals' and their practice will be assessed 'holistically'; you will need to demonstrate integration of all aspects of learning, and provide a sufficiency of evidence across all nine domains. The first of the nine domains of the PCF is:

Professionalism – Identify and behave as a professional social worker, committed to professional development

Professionalism, according to the PCF (1), should cover the following key areas.

- Recognising your own personal and professional boundaries – this includes your professional demeanour, ie, how you behave, how you communicate and show respect, your appearance as well as the boundaries you set with the adults, children and families you work with, regardless of setting.

- Recognising your own professional limitations, and how to seek advice.

- Identifying your learning needs; assuming responsibility for improving your practice including using supervision.

- Upholding and promoting the reputation of the profession.

It is OK to read about being a professional but you need to consider and understand what this really means to you. Why should you be a professional? How do you come across to your service users? What are the consequences if you are not acting appropriately? What are the implications for your actions and who does this affect? Here we try to answer some of these questions.

YOUR PROFESSIONAL IMAGE

As an NQSW it is important to:

- Consider your image – the way your colleagues, other professionals and service users view you.

- Be professional and positive and give the best image of yourself (and your service) you possibly can in a conscious and considered way. You can be energetic and enthusiastic but don't be over the top.

- Earn respect and people will listen to you and value your opinion. Think about how you communicate with people.

- Communicate clearly. Don't use jargon and words your audience won't understand, or words you don't even understand, just to try and look the part.

- Think about your mannerisms and your style, your voice, how you come across to others and your overall presence, but it is important you are still yourself. Think about what you wear. There is no real dress code but we would advise smart casual and be comfortable. You may want to check with your colleagues if denims/ jeans are acceptable for work. Also, if you are going to an important meeting you may want to 'dress up' a little or at least keep the 'smart' image rather than casual. If you are doing direct work with children and families you may want to dress down a little so that you are not coming across as 'stuffy' and 'unapproachable', as this can be a barrier to communicating with people. However, if you are in court there is a formal dress code, which for a woman could be a skirt or trouser suit and blouse, and for a man a suit and tie. Ask your colleagues if in doubt.

It is inevitable that sometimes you will be less confident and less self-assured. This is fine and it is to be expected that you will feel this way at different times throughout your journey along your ASYE; for example, the first time you go to court, chair a complex meeting or have to challenge someone perhaps more senior than you. Can you think of experiences at work or at home when you have perhaps felt very confident and other times when you have been less confident? How did it feel? How did you overcome this?

If you are feeling overwhelmed, maybe at having to speak in an important meeting, first of all don't panic, relax and take a deep breath and calm yourself down. Imagine you are at home and talking with a friend, you are in a familiar environment and you are relaxed. You could practise by sitting in front of a mirror in private and talking and familiarising yourself with how you sound and how you come across. But either way, don't worry about it, your confidence will grow with experience. If you are already confident, remember not to be big-headed as this can put people off. You will soon adopt your own style and image that suits you and works well and is appreciated by your colleagues and service users.

PROFESSIONAL RELATIONSHIPS

We spend a great deal of time at work, and in social work we deal with sensitive and difficult emotional situations, so it is not surprising that people become close to those they work with. People become important to you and friendships develop. Therefore, you need to be aware of boundaries within your relationships. It is not advisable to enter into an intimate relationship with a colleague, particularly in your team. However, if you do, you should ensure that this relationship does not impede your work. You should inform your line manager about the relationship so that they are aware of this as there may be a conflict of interest if you both work in the same team, or if one or other is in a senior position. It may be suggested that one of you leave the team and work elsewhere. Also, be aware of tension and pressures that starting a relationship with a colleague may have upon the team you work with. It may make others feel uncomfortable (www.workrelationships.co.uk). If the relationship ends or you have arguments this causes other difficulties and brings your personal life into the office. You are risking your professional reputation and career. In summary:

- don't be over-friendly and over-familiar with your colleagues;

- don't gossip about colleagues;

- ensure behaviour at work is professional and appropriate.

Look around the office and watch the behaviour of respected colleagues and you will soon learn what is appropriate and acceptable. See how people react when senior managers are around the office. This will give you some idea of expectations and office dynamics. Don't put yourself in a position you or others will be uncomfortable with.

SOCIAL MEDIA NETWORKS

It is important not only to consider your conduct while in work; you must also remember that, as a professional and a member of a professional body, you are under scrutiny at all times. Think about when you go out with your friends on a Saturday night. You have a few drinks and let your hair down. Yes that's fine but you MUST consider who may see you, what you are doing and that you are still representing the organisation you work for and your profession – especially if you socialise in an area close to your 'patch'. Unfortunately, you are never really off duty in that you are always answerable for your actions. This point is particularly important in the era of social media network sites such as Facebook as they can open up ethical dilemmas related to your professional conduct, conflicts of interests and issues around confidentiality for yourself, service users and your colleagues. Be aware that if you are on Facebook you may have a high security setting but your friends, who can see your account, may have lower settings, or be friends with others who are actually service users.

If you use Facebook, Twitter or any other social networking site, consider the information you give away about yourself on your personal profile and who has access to this and the implications:

- your date of birth;
- town or place where you live;
- information about your family or children;
- where you socialise and who with;
- personal photographs;
- your personal thoughts and feelings.

You also need to consider what you write on social media sites. You may post what you think are throwaway comments but be careful they can't be interpreted by others as unprofessional use of bias and derogatory language. All social workers have a responsibility to uphold public trust and confidence in social care services and must not behave in a way which would cause others to question their suitability to practise as a social worker.

Case Study – The trouble with Facebook

Jenny is a social worker who had worked in the team for approximately six months. Jenny and some of her colleagues went out to a friend's hen night at a club. The drinks were flowing and everyone was dancing. Jenny had too much to drink. Everyone was taking photos. One of the girls (not a social worker) pulled up her top and exposed her breasts in one of the photographs. Jenny and some of the social workers were included in this photo holding cocktail drinks, wearing silly hats and looking a little 'merry'. At the end of the evening Jenny, a little worse for wear and before going to bed, uploaded her photos onto Facebook for everyone to see what she thought was a great night out. Next morning, with a sudden realisation that she had uploaded totally unsuitable pictures, she removed them. However, on Monday, back in work, Jenny was greeted by angry colleagues and summoned to the manager's office, who had seen the pictures. Jenny was questioned about the events of the evening along with her colleagues and an internal investigation was carried out into the conduct of the social workers. She and the other social workers were very fortunate that the investigation found they had not breached any codes of conduct, and no further action was taken. However, Jenny's relationship with her colleagues was affected by her actions and she felt so uncomfortable she found it necessary to relocate to another team.

Have you ever been in any photographs where things could have been misconstrued or situations that may get you into trouble? As a qualified social worker you need to consider your actions in all aspects of your life and how this can impact upon your profession and your career as a social worker.

BOUNDARIES

Professional boundaries help safeguard you as a professional and your service users. It is easy to become 'attached' to service users, particularly when they are going through a difficult period in their lives. You need to be clear with service users about the parameters within which you work and set ground rules:

- the times that you will see service users;
- how long you will be working with them;
- known end dates if you are only going to work with them for a set period of time.

It is important to be clear from the outset with service users who you will share information about them with and the type of information you will share. Beware of giving service users information about yourself and your personal circumstances.

Your relationship with service users is very important but crossing the line can be very easy to do. Think about situations that you have been in where that could have happened. You must think about how the other person may perceive your helpful attitude and support. When a person is lonely and isolated and you spend time with them visiting to undertake a welfare check, they may perceive this as you being their 'friend' and not someone who is a paid professional doing their job. You can have empathy with people but it is important how this is communicated to your service users. Be aware of your body language too; for example, if a service user is upset and disclosing sensitive and personal information you should be aware of your posture. Sit facing the service user with open arms (not folded) so they can see you are receptive to what they have to say. Koprowska (2014) offers good insight into communication and interpersonal skills with service users.

If a service user gives you a gift – which is not to be encouraged – this must be declared to your line manager. Many organisations have procedures about declaring gifts and the value up to which you can accept a gift. This is usually around £5.

VALUES AND ETHICS

Understanding our values is a key requirement of social workers. The HCPC standards of proficiency 13 and 13.4 state that social workers must:

> **Understand key concepts of the knowledge base relevant to their profession [13] ... understand in relation to social work practice: the development and application of social work and social work values [13.4]**.

Alongside the Standards of Proficiency are the Standards of Conduct, Performance and Ethics (SCPEs) and in January 2016, the HCPC published their revised SCPEs. These standards are the *ethical framework* you must follow and abide by as a 'qualified social worker'. It is important you understand these, as they are used to assist the HCPC when making decisions about your character (and any other professionals who apply be registered with the HCPC) or should someone raise a concern about you or another registrant's practice. If you are a 'student' social worker you should read the 'Guidance on conduct and ethics for students', which sets out what the standards mean for you. These standards are not only for guiding professionals about the expectations of their role, but also the public can consult the standards to inform them what they can expect from health and care professionals. For more information, see www.hpc-uk.org/aboutregistration/standards/standardsofconductperformanceandethics/.

Your values shape the person that you are today; from the day you are born you are influenced by your parents and significant adults in your life and the experiences you had along

ACTIVITY · CROSSING THE LINE

Read these statements and consider whether the social worker is acting appropriately. Think about what you might do if your colleague was the social worker in this scenario.

○ A social worker works behind the bar of a club at the weekend.

○ A social worker works behind the bar of a club at the weekend. This club is a strip club.

○ A social worker is buying cigarettes for a 15-year-old boy they work with.

○ A male social worker is allowing a 16-year-old homeless girl to stay in his home. He is married and has children.

○ A single male social worker is allowing a homeless man from the hostel where he works to stay in his flat because the hostel is full.

○ A social worker is giving £10 a week to an elderly service user who does not have enough money after paying the rent to purchase food.

○ A social worker is taking £5 petrol money from a service user for taking them to a contact with their nephew. The journey is 45 miles and without a lift the service user would struggle to maintain the contact.

What did you decide to do? How would it make you feel if you knew some of this information about a colleague? Is it OK to ignore it?

Most of these statements could lead to a serious breach of conduct and are unacceptable, but there may be circumstances that you are unaware of or this may have been 'a one-off' situation. For example:

○ A social worker can work behind the bar of a club but it may not be acceptable to work in a club if their service users were customers as there would be a conflict of interest. It would certainly be 'crossing the line' to work in a strip club.

○ The social worker giving £10 a week to an elderly service user for food is not appropriate, but the social worker is probably just trying to help, and as a one-off may not lead to any disciplinary action. Instead the social worker should, for example, help the service user seek financial advice and get a review of their benefits.

If you have any concerns about a social work colleague who may be 'crossing the line' it is important that you discuss the issues with your line manager in the first instance as it is important they have all the facts about a situation. It could be that the social worker may just need some additional training as they are not aware of certain policies and procedures, but the social worker could have done something serious which should be reported as they may be breaching the HCPC's standards of proficiency.

your journey into adulthood – the schools you attended, the communities you lived in and the people you interact with on a day-to-day basis. You take these experiences into your working life and they help determine your decision making and your 'value' base for things you do.

As you work through your ASYE you will be given more responsibilities and complexities within your caseloads to broaden your knowledge and skills. You will be given more autonomy in your decision making until you have a greater knowledge base and increased accountability for assessments and decisions you make. However, you will need to continue to question your own values and ethics and the power imbalances between you and your service users. Be aware of assumptions that you make and understand the impact they may have upon your decision making, particularly when helping service users make informed decisions. For example, you are working with a teenage girl who becomes pregnant. She wants to talk to you about different options available to her, one of which is to terminate the pregnancy. You will have your own views and opinions about this, which have been shaped by your own upbringing, and experiences and beliefs. However, you cannot tell your service user it is wrong to have a termination although you may believe this yourself, or similarly you cannot encourage her to keep the baby because you believe this to be the right outcome. She must be given the opportunity to make an informed decision with all options explored, regardless of your own beliefs and values. Here your learning on placement and reflection, together with a clear understanding of professional boundaries versus your personal values and beliefs, will be invaluable.

If you believe you are not the right person to give advice, you should signpost the service user to the relevant agency. She may ask you to accompany her to the appointment and may feel that she does not want you to feel bad about her and the decision she reaches. You should tell her that you will support her regardless of her decision, and do not let your own opinions impact on the support you give her and her decision making. If you cannot do this you should consider raising this to your supervisor and perhaps consider handing the case to a colleague.

ACTIVITY · BEING AWARE OF YOUR VALUES

Write down a list of your own core values and ethics. These are those that you were brought up to believe and respect.

Now write down another list of your professional values and ethical base from which you practise and which uphold the reputation of the profession.

Think about how your own values have shaped you as a person and how they impact upon you as a social worker and your decision making. Are there certain decisions you would or would not make in your professional life that you would in your personal life and why? Is there any conflict? It's OK if there is, but you must think about how you will manage this conflict and ensure this does not impact on your professionalism.

In recent years, increased migration to the UK has meant there have been new influences from different cultures that impact upon us all. These changes affect the role of social work and the teaching of social work, and have wider implications for policies and procedures and legislation (Tovey, 2007). Therefore how we work with people from different communities and backgrounds will bring new ethical dilemmas to all social workers in each setting. As the world changes, social work has to move 'with the times'.

MORAL AND ETHICAL DILEMMAS

Case Study – Putting the pressure on

Leanne is a social worker within an adult social care learning difficulty team. She works with Dennis who is 58 years old and has a learning difficulty and mental health problems. Some years ago there were some concerns about Dennis's capacity. No formal assessment under the Mental Capacity Act was undertaken at that time, but of late he has seemed confused and his capacity has been brought into question once again. He lives alone with no family alive to help him make complex and difficult decisions and is reliant upon Leanne for this type of support. Dennis does not have an IMCA (Independent Mental Capacity Advocate). Dennis is newly diagnosed with cancer and during Leanne's visit he tells her he is not going to accept treatment and he is frightened. Leanne has a close working relationship with Dennis and is upset by the news and Dennis's decision. Leanne believes that Dennis should accept the treatment as this will give him a few more years. Dennis tells Leanne to cancel his hospital appointments and that he will not go for any treatment and refuses to talk to her about this when she pushes the issue. Leanne returns to the office and rings the hospital but confirms that Dennis will be attending his next appointment in a week's time and that he wishes to go ahead with the treatment and she will bring him along to the appointment. Leanne's personal belief is that all life is precious and under no circumstances can you refuse treatment that will promote chances of life. Her father is a cancer survivor and is in remission. Leanne visits Dennis every day for the next week, and puts pressure on Dennis to go to the appointment. Eventually Dennis attends the appointment and reluctantly agrees to have the initial stage of the treatment to have a biopsy and a lump removed.

What would you have done and why? What advice would you have given Dennis? What are the ethical and moral issues versus the legalities of Leanne's actions? Consider Dennis's mental capacity; should this have been reassessed? Is Leanne's manager at fault? (See Chapter 9.)

There are many 'moral' issues that social workers face, and it is not always easy to establish the right or wrong answers to many situations, particularly when these are complex. Therefore, it is important to be critical in your thinking and to widen the discussion about 'moral' issues and 'ethical dilemmas' and discuss them with your supervisor, practice educator and/or other professionals who may be involved with your service user (Tovey, 2007). As an NQSW it is important not to feel overwhelmed with some of these difficult decisions. In supervision you should reflect upon your own standpoint, and understand why you feel the way you do about your decision making.

If some of these decisions or situations you find yourself in are too close to a personal experience or belief, you may not wish to be faced with this situation in your work and should consider a different service user group. Your relationship with your service user must remain professional and have clear boundaries in place.

FEEDBACK

It is essential to get feedback, either as an organisation or as an individual. It helps us learn about what we are doing well and what is working, but also highlights the things we could do better and improve upon.

Service user feedback

Local authorities have promoted more service user 'participation' and are increasingly involving service users in shaping services within their communities. This is a positive step forward in breaking down some of the barriers with service users and taking on board their thoughts and opinions when making decisions about where funding is spent.

As a social worker it is important to continually seek feedback from service users and work in 'partnership' with them. As part of your ASYE you will be observed within your practice including with your service users so that your manager can assess your progress and report back to you. In this circumstance you may be able to choose the service user you are visiting during your observation and have a good idea that their feedback will be positive. However, you must remember that there is a balance of power that is often tipped in your favour as a professional and it is important this power imbalance does not influence what the service user has to say.

Don't worry if they are not positive about you as a worker. They may not really be upset with you, but rather because they did not get the outcomes they wanted. It is still important, however, to find out about the process that they went through and how this is working or where changes need to be made (College of Social Work, 2012, pp 1–3). People experience things differently but the process should be the same; therefore it is essential that everyone is treated fairly and equally. The timing of obtaining feedback may not be ideal and there are different variables that would affect this, but nevertheless the opportunity should be made available as it is a valuable way of assessing both the services on offer and your professionalism.

Feedback from colleagues

You can seek feedback from colleagues within your team. Perhaps you could co-work cases with peers where appropriate or do joint visits and ask your colleagues to give you some constructive feedback. You will also receive feedback from your supervisor within your supervision. Here you will be reflecting upon your experiences with service users and therefore you should consider how you have taken feedback from your service users and what you have learned from this.

Obtaining feedback

There are different ways to get feedback, including:

* giving questionnaires;
* suggestion boxes;
* feedback forms;
* holding face-to-face reviews;
* asking colleagues.

CHANGING OURSELVES AND CHALLENGING OTHERS

It is important that you learn about yourself from others and accept constructive criticism, seeking a broader understanding of a situation by reflecting on your skills and your own models of social work and how you practise. We will discuss in Chapter 9 how we are often in conflict about our pre-existing beliefs, 'cognitive dissonance' (Festinger, 1957). At times we will have to accept that we are not always right and make efforts to change (we discuss 'change' in Chapter 7).

As a professional you must be open to change and accept the opinions of others, even if your personal view and assumptions are different. This will ensure that the service user is kept at the centre of your practice. In order to change and be able to manage others through change, you need to understand your attitude towards change (Martin et al., 2010). To help you do this:

* keep up to date with changes within your organisation;
* keep your skills and knowledge up to date, including those within your profession;
* be aware of how change affects your emotional well-being.

'The Ladder of Inference', created by Chris Argyris and used by Peter Senge (2006), is a great tool to ensure our actions and decisions are based on reality when we either need to change our view or challenge other people's conclusions. Senge (2006) states there are seven rungs on his ladder:

1. We adopt our own beliefs by making conclusions about what we have experienced and observed.
2. We interpret what this means to us.
3. We affix meaning.
4. We make our assumptions.
5. We arrive at a conclusion based on the assumption and our interpretation of the fact.
6. We develop a belief.
7. We take action based on what we believe is correct.

Let's look at an example of this in practice. You are giving a presentation at a staff meeting and you notice that a colleague is checking a message on their phone. Immediately you add meaning to this by assuming that they are not interested in what you are saying (you did not notice they were showing interest prior to their message alert). What you also do not know is that they are on duty and must check their phone. You make an assumption they are bored. You conclude that everyone is bored and your presentation has not gone very well and no one has confidence in you. You take action based on your conclusion and decide you are not going to do any more presentations. By doing this you have not considered all the positives in your presentation and that everyone actually thought it was very well presented and informative.

Therefore, in order to improve communication and help change your own or challenge others' points of view, use the ladder of inference, linking the seven rungs on the ladder with reflective practice:

- Reflect – on what are you basing your assumptions and decisions?
- Share your thoughts and communicate with others – ask is the information correct?
- Inquire and clarify thoughts of others involved – have you have reached the right conclusion and validated your decisions before taking action?

As an NQSW you may be afraid to challenge others but remember you are a professional in your own right and have earned the right to be acknowledged and respected. You should feel confident to challenge others but do your research first, checking out as much information as you can to add credibility to your argument, and to help influence other professionals to accept your viewpoint and to show you have taken the time to find out about the subject first. However, you must also appreciate the expertise of those around you and your own strengths and limitations. When challenging others this must be done in a professional, mature way and at the appropriate time. Be prepared for the response that you may get as others challenge you. You have to earn respect from colleagues and ensure that you are challenging in an appropriate way and in the right forum.

Maximising your professional capabilities **33**

Your new habits

Now you have considered your values, ethics and boundaries and have learned how to be the best you can, why not start using your new habits immediately?

Your Toolkit – Think about your values and ethics and how they may impact upon your decision making and advice you may give to service users. Consider how you will manage boundaries and receive feedback. Think about how you may address any issues with your line manager. Record any evidence for your assessment.

TAKING IT FURTHER

Judd, RG, Johnston, LB (2012) Ethical Consequences of Using Social Network Sites for Students in Professional Social Work Programs. Journal of Social Work Values and Ethics, 9(1): 5–12

Koprowska, J (2014) Communication and Interpersonal Skills in Social Work, 4th edn. London: Learning Matters

Oko, J (2012) Understanding and Using Theory in Social Work, 2nd edn, Chapters 3 and 4. Exeter: Learning Matters

Senge, P (2006) The Fifth Discipline: The Art and Practice of The Learning Organization, 2nd edn. Random House Business

Website*:*

www.workrelationships.co.uk

4 Working out 'where you are at'

INTRODUCTION

This chapter will help you recognise 'where you are at' in terms of your own developmental journey through your ASYE. We will look at ways of identifying your current position and of managing some of the issues that may arise. By the end of the chapter you will be aware of your own vulnerabilities, your strengths and the areas in which you need to make changes. We will show you how to undertake a SWOT analysis on yourself and the latter part of the chapter will demonstrate how you can use this tool to help manage your cases and see 'where you are at' with some of the concerns you may have.

- ○ Why do I need to know 'where I am at'?
- ○ SWOT analysis – 'with a difference'
- ○ Bringing SWOT and SWOB into your practice
- ○ Feedback

Links to:

PCF 1 – Professionalism

PCF 2 – Values and Ethics

PCF 4 – Rights, Justice and Economic Well-being

PCF 5 – Knowledge

PCF 6 – Critical Reflection and Analysis

PCF 7 – Intervention and Skills

WHY DO I NEED TO KNOW 'WHERE I AM AT'?

It is essential to be aware of how particular aspects of our personal lives can impact upon our working lives; and to know how to deal with this and, where possible, effectively separate the two or reach a manageable and acceptable crossover. We may call these issues our 'vulnerabilities'. Vulnerability comes in many forms and is different for everyone, at different times in our lives. It is part of our natural emotional state and we experience this, for example, when we lose a loved one – we feel susceptible and are often at our lowest ebb. However, being aware of our own vulnerabilities can make us stronger and assist us to develop defences to help us manage our lives and be positive. It is not a bad thing, as long as we recognise and accept them, understand the emotional impact they have upon us and build resilience in order to manage our vulnerabilities. Suppressing our emotions can result in stress and depression.

We all have things going on in our private lives at times that make our working lives more difficult, but unfortunately we are not able to say 'I'm not coming into work for a few weeks until I sort out my problems'. We therefore have to juggle things around and put contingencies in place. Some of these difficulties may be:

- our health – this may be physical or mental health;
- caring for sick or elderly relatives;
- caring for a sick or disabled child;
- managing childcare or childcare between ex-partners (shared care arrangements).

In addition to this there are many other practical issues that may arise such as having to deal with a burst pipe, or our car breaking down. Whatever it is we are all vulnerable at different times. These things will and do impact upon our working lives.

In order to avoid your own vulnerabilities impacting upon your work you will need strategies for dealing with them and we will offer you a number to consider.

ACTIVITY • MY VULNERABILITIES

- ○ Think about your personal life for a few moments and consider where you are most vulnerable. How may some of these vulnerabilities cross over into your working life?
- ○ Now make a list using three columns and write down your vulnerabilities, how they impact upon your job and how you can manage this. See the example below to get you started.

Personal life	*Impact on work*	*How will I manage this?*
I have three children each attending different schools	This may mean I will be late occasionally	Ask manager re flexitime, good routines, support from other parents

The vulnerabilities within our personal lives are something that we have to manage and no doubt at different times in our lives these will change, and how they impact upon our working lives will vary too. Many you will deal with without any problem. However, you may wish to inform your manager about any that you know are a particular issue, for example, a sick child, so that they are aware of what you are coping with and how this may impact upon your working life. If necessary, discuss with your manager the possibility of needing time off or of having some flexibility in terms of working hours. It is much better to be open and honest about vulnerabilities that may impact upon your work. However, you will soon learn to manage them and overcome the smaller issues in your life without too much problem.

As a student or NQSW you have probably felt vulnerable at different times along your journey into social work, and will no doubt have times when you will continue to do so. Think about your first day at university. How did you feel? Perhaps you felt vulnerable at some stage during your first week – unsure of what you were doing, thinking everyone else was OK and it was just you that was scared but also excited. Yes, you had some vulnerabilities.

ACTIVITY • MY FIRST WEEK AS AN NQSW

Think about your vulnerabilities during your first week(s) as you enter your new job as an employee or as a student on placement. We have suggested three headings to get you thinking, and an example.

Work issues	*Impact on you*	*How will I manage it?*
Not knowing my way around	Feel inadequate, getting lost	Ask for help, get a map

---

Now, we will focus on ways you can address some of the ongoing issues within your role and look at a tool you can use to put this down on paper and make plans to move forward (although you can adapt these techniques in all areas of your life). Once you have identified your vulnerabilities, it is essential to also know your strengths and areas for improvement. For the purpose of the next section we will call your areas for improvement 'weaknesses' but please don't feel that you are weak – it's only terminology used around the theory. By being aware of your strengths and weaknesses you will be aware of how best to approach the challenges that lie ahead. We often think it is easy to recognise the things that we are not so good at, or the things we do not do so well – often there are enough people that will all too quickly point out the negatives. However, it is not always easy to know what we are good at. It may seem obvious but we don't often know how well we are doing or what our strengths are – often we just get on with things. Therefore, it is important to reflect on your strengths and weaknesses and to know 'where you are at'. This will be a changing theme as you develop in different areas along your journey through your ASYE. In order to help you with this we invite you to look at a SWOT analysis – with a difference.

SWOT ANALYSIS – 'WITH A DIFFERENCE'

SWOT analysis is a strategic planning tool that is used to evaluate the key internal and external factors that are important in trying to reach a predefined objective. The internal factors are divided into *Strengths* and *Weaknesses*, and the external into *Opportunities* and *Threats*, hence the name (Maylor, 2005). The technique is credited to Albert Humphrey, who led a convention at the Stanford Research Institute (now SRI International) in the 1960s and 1970s (http://en.wikipedia.org/wiki/SWOT_analysis). As stated, a SWOT is usually used at a strategic level; however, we've decided to use it at a more personal level to allow you as a worker to look at yourself. Below is an example completed by us when we were employed as agency social workers, ie, not as permanent employees.

SWOT analysis – agency social worker

Strengths	Weaknesses
Social worker can gain experience in lots of areas	Lack of equipment – get what's left
Social worker can be paid weekly	Having to learn new IT systems
Builds confidence and assertiveness	Lots of moving from one place to another
Not having to be involved in 'office politics'	Supervision – not always seen as priority
Money for introducing a friend to the agency	Have to 'budget' for holidays/leave
Gain good reputation and return to places	No sick pay; 'no work no pay'
Confident worker	Expected to 'hit the ground running'
Gets on with different people/people at different levels	No support for newly qualified agency social worker
Enjoys responsibility/using own initiative	Less commitment to organisation

Opportunities	Threats
Social worker has lots of opportunities to work in different organisations	Current climate causes uncertainty
Learn new skills/new service user groups	Permanent jobs at risk
Social worker can leave without long notice period	First to go when organisation making cuts
Work for your own company	Hot desking
You have more control over your career choices	Staff may resent agency worker's perceived 'higher' salary
Interview process quick and easy when changing jobs	Lack of support from within organisation
Have skills and can work abroad with them	Agency doesn't understand your role
	No local authority pension scheme

When working out 'where you are at' a SWOT is a useful tool to use. Think about:

- Your strengths – things you are good at. Even if you can't think of things your colleagues can no doubt think of lots of positive things about you. Think about positive experiences and outcomes you have had and what has worked well, and also your support networks around you – colleagues, peers, support groups and other areas where support is available such as the internet and books and journals. Think about the resources that you have access to. Think about skills you have and how you have utilised these well.

- Your weaknesses – don't be too hard on yourself but be honest. Think of areas where you may need additional support. Think about weaknesses such as lack of resources, or things that may be impacting upon the situation that is causing a weakness. Consider difficult situations or relationships that may be a weak link. Think about relationships and their weaknesses, such as communication difficulties, disability or social isolation.

- Think about your physical working environment – this may be both a strength and a weakness.

- Opportunities – think about opportunities that are available to you to move things forward. Some of these may interlink in other areas such as strengths. Think about resources available and future planning and skills you have. Look at how universal services may be able to support you, particularly anything free – local libraries, carers centres, volunteer services. Think about the community and what this could offer to support. Think about areas for positive change for yourself, work opportunities or courses available, either work experience or educational courses. Practical things.

- Threats – think what the impact might be if the opportunities are not achieved or if things fail, the consequences for you and the situation you are in. Consider if relationships break down and impact upon the situation. Health – threat if single carer is ill, etc.

ACTIVITY • SWOT

Write down the four headings, Strengths, Weaknesses, Opportunities and Threats, and complete a SWOT for yourself based on your role. Think about the different headings and what they mean to you and your circumstances.

When you have done that, *and not before*, compare your SWOT with the one below. This is a SWOT carried out by a student social worker, at the end of her first placement, on a first year Master's course. You can complete a SWOT regardless of age and experience, and whatever role and situation you are in. This is very brief, but gives you some ideas.

Strengths
Prior knowledge and experience
Commitment/determination
Transferable skills

Weaknesses
Fear of getting things wrong
Emotional involvement

Opportunities
Innovation and systems change
Personal and professional development

Threats
Organisational constraints and boundaries
'Workload' and stress/Family crisis
Unsupportive practice educator

You cannot think of everything but think of what may be relevant to the current situation.

As a result of completing the exercise the student was able to identify her strengths and was able to write a 'new lone working policy' transferring her knowledge and experience from a previous job. She also discussed the areas for development (weaknesses) with her practice educator to look at ways of overcoming these within her placement.

BRINGING SWOT AND SWOB INTO YOUR PRACTICE

In social work we come across many people who are vulnerable. This may be a service user or a member of their family. They are vulnerable for different reasons, such as a learning difficulty, a mental health problem or as the result of abuse, and you need to learn to help them manage their vulnerabilities as you do yours.

We will now look at how you can adapt the SWOT and bring this into your work in a different way. You can use this within your practice and case management.

You can adapt the SWOT to use with your cases but perhaps consider this to be a 'SWOB', which may be your *Strengths* and *Weaknesses* for managing the case and what *Outcomes* you are trying to achieve with the family and the *Barriers* to this. Or you may also want to switch this to *Strengths* and *Weaknesses* perhaps of the family unit, versus *Objectives* that they are trying to achieve and *Blocks* that are preventing the family from meeting the objectives. You could choose whichever words best suit the situation.

ACTIVITY • SWOB

○   Have a go at doing a SWOB for one of your cases. Think about your strengths and weaknesses as a worker and perhaps what objectives/ outcomes you have for the case and what is blocking you from meeting those objectives. Think about the vulnerabilities involved in each case.

○   Now have a go at doing a SWOB for a family you are working with but from their perspective. Think of their strengths and weaknesses and then the outcomes/objectives or blocks/barriers to overcoming the issues.

This will then give you a clear picture of 'where you are at' in terms of the case management and 'where the family are at' and what you and/or the family may need to do in order to move things forward. This is a 'snapshot' of a situation and can be done at different times.

This type of activity will help you to keep focused on your desired outcomes and stay neutral and remain professional so that you can clearly see 'where you are at' and see where 'your service users are at'. You can see the presenting issues for everyone. Think about the dynamics when you are looking at planning and moving forward. Think about how the relationships interlink and the family dynamics. You could add a 'P' for *Professional* influences that impact upon the case, ie from others involved such as consultants, physiotherapists, occupational therapists, speech and language therapists, and how these professionals may impact on your decision making. Also, consider areas of conflict of interests or challenges; for example, a case may involve a social worker from adult social care working with a parent and a social worker for a child and their priorities may conflict. This will help you develop a clear understanding of agencies and/ or services involved with your families or service users. Think about how you may manage this type of conflict and what influences this may have on how you would manage the case and overcome any challenges. Each time you do a SWOT or SWOB, you must consider legislation and policies and procedures that may impact upon your case and decision making.

You can create 'acronyms' for any area of your social work or your case management. We call this the 'acronym theory'; we sometimes also call it PACRONYM – when we are adding in P for 'Protection' or 'Protective factors'.

A   Assessing current situation
C   Considering impact on/of others
R   Risk management
O   Outcome focused
N   New ways forward for self/others
Y   Yourself – find out 'where you are at'
M   Measuring progress

You may want to develop this system for a case where there is a risk of significant harm. You can just jot down the different aspects that you want to think about. You may want to consider Risk of harm (*Risk*), How you want to Manage the risk (*Manage*), Positives for family or protective factors (*Positives* or *Protectors*) and finally what external Support is in place or available (*Support*) – forming the acronym *RMPS*. You could sit down with your service users and complete one of these with them so that they are aware of your concerns, how they can address these concerns and what support is in place to help them do this.

This method will help you develop your confidence and understanding as you work towards becoming a more emotionally intelligent social worker (see Chapter 5). It will also give you an awareness of where you may require additional support or training within your continuing professional development or case management. You could also do this within supervision with your manager to help see what is going on in your cases.

This is a simple and easy way to break down some of the issues that you face as a social worker, particularly with complex cases. It will often help you come to decisions and help you manage the vulnerabilities, difficulties on the cases and your own or service users' strengths and weaknesses.

Case Study – An acronym in action

Jag was a newly qualified social worker for a local authority. There was an ongoing concern about a girl on her caseload who was having relationships with inappropriate adult males and going missing for days. Jag was unsure how to deal with the issues and was due to have supervision with her manager the next day. In order to prepare for the supervision and to show her manager that she had given consideration to the presenting issues and to demonstrate her learning, Jag thought about the different aspects of the case and decided to use the 'acronym theory'. Having considered it some more, she concluded that RMPS – Risks, Management, Protectors and Support were the factors she needed to consider:

o   *Risks – child absconding with adult males, going missing for days, risk of sexual exploitation.*

o   *Management – may need 'Stay Safe' Meeting or Child Protection Conference, etc. – her manager would advise; discuss in supervision sessions; report child missing to police and out of hours; use other agencies; pick up and drop off child when she goes out where necessary. Put risk assessment in place.*

o   *Protectors – parents very supportive; school aware; police involved; Barnardo's worker involved and Missing Persons scheme involved. 'Working Together' (Department for Education, 2015). Policy and Procedures/Legislation.*

o   *Support – good supportive team manager and support from Principal Social Worker; regular discussions and visits to family. Family have support networks.*

Jag was able to take the information to her manager and they agreed a plan in order to put strategies in place to help safeguard the child. They did discuss some further issues that Jag had not considered but her manager was very pleased that Jag had given the case consideration and she knew 'where she was at' with her case.

SIGNS OF SAFETY

Some of you may have experience of working with the Signs of Safety Model which has been adopted by many local authorities across the UK over recent years, and also in many countries across the world. Signs of Safety is a Solution and Safety Orientated Approach to Child Protection Case Work, which was founded by Andrew Turnell and

Steve Edwards circa 1999. This approach is an excellent model for 'working out where you are at' with your families and involves them finding their own solutions to the problems in their lives while working with professionals but taking a 'family approach' and the family coming up with their own 'safety plan'.The approach uses danger statements and safety goals in plain and simple language that the children and family can understand and scores everyone's worries. If you are familiar with this approach you can use our SWOT and/or SWOB and other acronyms you have come up with, with this model to help you find out *where you are at* with your cases. We are sure by using these models together and with families or on your own it will help to achieve positive outcomes and clear next steps.

FEEDBACK

Another way of assessing *where you are at* is to ask for feedback. There are two types of feedback – formative or summative (Tovey, 2007).

Formative is the type of feedback that you can get from your colleagues, peers and from your manager. During your ASYE you will receive regular feedback in supervision, and hopefully from your colleagues about your development, and you can use this to inform yourself of how best to improve your practice, and plan your continuing professional development. Again, your manager will help you with this and it should be discussed in supervision (see Chapter 9). You can get feedback from service users and there are different ways you can approach this, ie questionnaire, feedback forms, direct discussion though you need to be sensitive when approaching people (see Chapter 3 for further discussion).

Summative feedback is formal feedback, for example, that given in report form from your practice educator or supervisor after submitting your portfolio. This is usually an assessed piece of work. This type of feedback will often give recommendations on how to improve your work or point you to other areas of research you may wish to consider that may improve your practice. Recommendations may be made about other areas of study that you can pursue or aspects of your work that you may want to consider working towards. You will no doubt remember this type of feedback from your tutors at university when you receive your assignments back telling you if you have passed or failed.

Your new habits

Think about your key learning from this chapter and how you will change your practice and put this into action – what will you do differently? Go on … give it a try! Try out some of your own acronyms and consider how you can use these in different areas of your work.

 Your Toolkit – Identify your personal vulnerabilities and how they may impact on your work, then decide how you may wish to address these as you progress. Next, add these to your Toolkit along with your strengths and any areas you have for your development.

TAKING IT FURTHER

Calder, CM (2016) Risk in Child Protection. Assessment Challenges and Frameworks for Practice. London: Jessica Kingsley Publishers

Fine, LG (2010) The SWOT Analysis: Using Your Strength to Overcome Weaknesses, Using Opportunities to Overcome Threats (http://en.wikipedia.org/wiki/SWOT_analysis)

Hothersall, SJ, Maas-Lowit, M (2010) Need, Risk and Protection in Social Work Practice. Exeter: Learning Matters (Chapter 1, Need and Vulnerability; Chapter 2, Risk)

Larkin, M (2009) Vulnerable Groups in Health and Social Care. London: Sage

Turnell, A, Edwards, S (1999) Signs of Safety: A Solution and Safety Oriented Approach to Child Protection Casework.

5 Developing your emotional intelligence

INTRODUCTION

There is an increasing recognition that people who have high levels of emotional intelligence (EI) are more successful in relationships and in their chosen career. This chapter provides a basic introduction to the concept of emotional intelligence and, by presenting it within a framework, seeks to help you with the development of knowledge and skill in this area.

The chapter begins with a look at the origins of EI, before we move on to encourage you to test your own EI levels, and to look at strategies for improvement and how this can help your relationships and success both in and out of the workplace.

EI is a fairly easy concept to understand and includes many of the things that you will have learned in university. Improving your own EI levels should enable you to become a more effective practitioner.

o   What is EI?
o   How can you develop your EI levels?
o   Understanding and using the concept of EI in social work
o   Assessing your EI levels
o   Getting in touch with your feelings
o   How can your EI be improved?
o   How does improving our EI improve our effectiveness?
o   EI and social work, values and ethics
o   Stress and EI
o   Resilience

Links to:

PCF 2 – Values and Ethics

PCF 3 – Diversity

PCF 4 – Rights, Justice and Economic Well-being

PCF 5 – Knowledge

PCF 7 – Intervention and Skills

PCF 8 – Contexts and Organisations

WHAT IS EMOTIONAL INTELLIGENCE?

If we (the authors) were to describe EI we would say that, simply put, it entails

> *Developing an understanding of your own and others' emotions and using that knowledge to direct your thinking and respond more appropriately.*

The great news is that EI is not complicated to understand and does not rely on your understanding of any detailed theoretical frameworks or concepts. Rather, you should find it quite easy to apply what you learn here to yourself and to your behaviour and then to learn how to evaluate this and to respond to other people.

When we think of the word 'intelligence', this is usually linked to cognition or cognitive intelligence, ie the way that we *think* about things. Usually we talk about an individual's 'IQ' or 'intelligence quotient' and this has long been understood and can be measured by standardised testing. There is a great deal written about our cognitive abilities and a well-established understanding that the greater our cognitive abilities, the greater success we may have in life. A Google search using both the terms 'emotional intelligence' and 'cognitive intelligence' reveals more than three times as many references to 'cognitive' as to 'emotional' intelligence.

Emotional intelligence (EI, or sometimes also referred to as 'EQ') is a relatively new term and relates to the way that we *feel* about things. Anything related to our emotions and our emotional development is more difficult to define and therefore to understand. It is not something that is easily measured or tested and one of the reasons for this is that it is a subjective ideology which is subject to many complex variables.

The earliest discussion around our emotional abilities in this context appeared in Thorndike (1920), when the term 'social intelligence' was used to define people who are socially adaptable and who have a good insight and sensitivity. It was not until the mid-1980s that Payne introduced the term 'emotional intelligence'.

Following this in 1990, Salovey and Mayer put forward the theory that people who understood their own emotions, and were able to use this to positively respond to others around them, were enabled to develop a high level of social skills. This approach caught popular attention and led to a rash of research on the subject that continues to this day.

However, it was Goleman (1995) who argued that emotional intelligence was every bit as important as our cognitive intelligence. He identified a number of qualities (eg impulse control, motivation, persistence) which would enable individuals to lead a well-balanced, successful and fulfilled life. He posited that emotional ability may be more important than cognitive ability in the quest for success. Following this the term 'emotional intelligence' was embraced by many in the business world, became widely accepted and has since been used to develop individuals, teams and workforces the world over.

More recently (and perhaps more specifically for us), Howe (2008) has written about 'emotionally intelligent social workers' and discusses in depth the links that can be made between the development of social workers' EI and how this can help to improve efficiency in practice.

In 1997, following their earlier work, Salovey and Mayer introduced their four-branch model in which they define EI as the ability to:

*   accurately perceive emotions in oneself and others;
*   use emotions to facilitate thinking;
*   understand emotional meanings; and
*   manage emotions.

So, if we can interpret (via our cognitive ability) correctly the thoughts and feelings of ourselves and others and use this information to inform our own thoughts, we can be enabled and empowered to understand, and respond appropriately to both our own and others' needs.

As you can see, EI is a fairly simple notion and though this may be relatively new to you, you will definitely already know the basics. What we aim to do here is to explore the issues a little further, to encourage you to acknowledge and understand your own thoughts, feelings, emotions and behaviours and those of others, and to get you to delve a little bit deeper below the surface. That should be quite easy for social workers, as that is what we are trained to do – but we sometimes do not apply what we learn to ourselves. Let's start by looking at where you are at just now – before we go any further, check your current EI levels by completing the simple activity below. This is not meant to be an exact science, more a guide and an introduction to get you to think about your own levels of EI.

It is important to be able to acknowledge and appreciate your emotions, including those of happiness, sadness, fear and joy, and then to understand how they connect with and impact on your actions. It is also vital to express your emotions, and to recognise the emotional toil and the psychological and behavioural consequences of not doing so and to build in some self-regulation. Those of us who are not conscious of our emotions or who try and dull them, perhaps due to previous negative experiences, may well have less of an ability to appreciate their own or others' emotions and this can have a serious impact upon their actions and communication. Social workers need to have good communication skills alongside self-confidence in order to get the most from their assessments and also in order to challenge others appropriately in the course of their work.

ACTIVITY • TESTING MY OWN EI LEVELS

Rate your EI skills on a scale of 1–5, where 1 is 'never' and 5 is 'always'.

1. I am honest when I think about how my behaviour and responses impact on others.
2. I am aware of my feelings at any given time.
3. I am able to be in control of my emotions.
4. I am able to view things from the other's perspective.
5. I have good social skills.
6. I accept others for who and what they are.
7. I relish challenge and know what I want from life.
8. I have fun and laugh with others.
9. I consider myself part of a greater team called humanity.
10. I am open to relationships with others.

Add up your score and see where you are at:

0–16: Oh dear – read on and you will move up the scores, no doubt; come back and test yourself again in a month.

17–30: Not bad – but room for improvement here.

31–40: Good – you are on the right track but could probably learn a thing or two.

Over 40: Move to the top of the class – this is excellent, but you may still find this chapter beneficial as a refresher.

Place yourself on the scale below and think about the areas you would like to improve.

My EI scale:

Oh dear — Not bad — Good — Top of the class — Off the scale

Your previous learning will have included communication skills – observing, listening and ensuring a clear spoken word. It will have included the skills of reflection and analysis, and you will have an appreciation of positivity, tolerance, an acceptance of others, and the importance of independence rather than dependence. All of these are important when thinking about EI.

Case Study – The authors (!)

As we were developing this simple test we decided to try it out for ourselves.

Angie felt that she had pretty high levels of EI and after all had done most of the work on this chapter. She considers that she is an open and responsive person with pretty good self-awareness and social skills – she scored 31 – which was about right. She recognised that she could still improve in areas and had already identified that at times she could be too serious and not have enough fun in life.

Julie found she had a high level of EI, scoring 41, although prior to doing research for this chapter she didn't realise how much we use and draw upon our EI as social workers. Julie felt she was able to have fun and laugh with others and she accepts people for who they are but she scored lower at knowing what she wants from life and this is an area for her development – before it's too late!

Matzke (2012) puts forward the following 12 points as a basis for the development of EI. (There are many other examples of qualities that make up positive EI; this is one example.)

1. *Openness* – opening ourselves to others and to new experiences and having the ability to learn from these experiences. Having an open and enquiring mind and the ability to express ourselves clearly and be alive to all possibilities.

2. *Acceptance* – a feeling of worthiness and value towards ourselves and others' thoughts, needs, feelings and opinions. But also an acceptance that life includes limitations.

3. *Spontaneity* – the enjoyment of life and of grasping each opportunity that is presented, having fun and avoiding controlling all around us.

4. *Autonomy* – becoming an independent person, who is able to take responsibility and be accountable and to make choices, to take risks and make mistakes.

5. *Trusting relationships* – the ability to engage with others and to care for and be cared for and to enjoy intimate relationships.

6. *Fellowship with humanity* – a feeling of being a part of community and society and of being a part of a larger group who are similar and at the same time, unique.

7. *A sense of humour* – (don't we all need this?) the ability to laugh at ourselves and with others appropriately and to see the funnier side of life. To enjoy a lightness of spirit.

8. *Living here and now* – enjoying the moment and not seeking to dwell on the past or anticipate or plan the future too much.

9. *Sense of awe and wonder* – looking around and enjoying what life and the world has to offer, knowing and appreciating that pleasure is to be found in the simple things in life.

10. *Tolerance for ambiguity* – having the ability to understand that not all things are clear cut, or black and white, and that sometimes there are no simple answers to life's problems.

11. *Sense of balance and harmony* – being able to fully engage with others and with life and having a sense of wholeness and of being fulfilled by life's experiences.

12. *Affirmative life attitudes* – having plans and goals in life and striving for them, having the drive and working hard to succeed and to engage in challenging pursuits.

In essence these are the areas that we need to develop in order to enhance our own levels of EI. Think about yourself and how you can relate to what Matzke suggests. Think about how the above relates to the values and ethics that are expected of you as a social worker. You should be able to see the similarities here, for example, the notion of 'acceptance' is fundamental to the work of a social worker. Study the list and see which others you can see.

Can you link yourself and your own behaviour to the list above? Are there areas you would like to improve in? Do you agree with the above or can you see things that are missing? This is not a definitive list; EI levels will be slightly different for us all, at different times. The idea of us all having perfectly developed EI skills that allow us to be in tune with ourselves and others all of the time may be a little idealistic, but this is a starting point and something to strive for.

How can you develop your EI levels?

The first thing we are going to do is to get back to basics and put you in touch with your feelings.

ACTIVITY • GETTING IN TOUCH WITH YOUR FEELINGS

Think about a recent working day and imagine your journey from waking up to lunch time. Remember what was happening in detail and how the morning went, who was involved in it, how it went, was it typical or atypical? Try to close your eyes and recall as much as you can.

List the feelings that you had when:

o   you first woke up and were getting ready for work;
o   you were driving in to and arriving at work;
o   when you opened your diary and as you went about the day's work.

Think about both positive and negative feelings and think about the interactions these led to and how you managed these. Next, try to think about these within the context of the 12 points above and of Salovey and Mayer's theory. Explore your thoughts, feeling and behaviour. What does this tell you about where you were at this morning? The aim of the activity is to put you in touch with your feelings and link this to the things that we know can enhance your EI.

Having read so far and gained a basic understanding of the concept of EI, we hope that you will want to move forward. Even those of us that think we have it worked out can learn and develop and the continuation of your journey starts here. One other thing to remember about developing your own EI level is that it can benefit you, not only as a worker but as an individual and the skills you learn will be invaluable from now on in all areas of your life. We would suggest that the following may be useful in your development:

1.   Read around the subject

This chapter is an introduction to a fascinating subject, but is only the start of your journey. There are many great books around, some of which are listed below, and the internet is a great resource for research. Allow yourself to spend some time on this.

2.   Attend training

As the subject of EI is more widely understood, courses are being offered and we have heard of some excellent ones. This gives you the chance to gain knowledge and understanding and to learn and share with others as you develop. If there are no courses locally, ask your organisation if they can find or develop one. Add this to your training needs list.

3.   Know where you are at

Having taken our test, you should have a clearer idea of how good your EI skills are and the areas that you would like to improve; this together with your reading will improve your understanding and give you ideas for moving forward. You can always retest yourself at any point and compare your scores.

4.   Watch others and see how they respond to you

A great way to gain an insight into your own EI levels is to learn from others. You will no doubt anticipate a certain response from others. Is this always what you expect? Sometimes? Always? Never? Why is this, and is this consistent? Examining our inter-actions with others can be a great learning experience. You were taught to do this in journals during your training – but extend this and look at this specifically in the context of wanting to develop your EI skills and see what happens. You may be quite amazed at the results. Remember – 'it's not what you say, but how you say it'.

5.   Ask for feedback

This is another great way to learn and develop. Choose someone you trust and ask them for feedback on the way that they see you and how you respond to others. Is this the same as you see yourself? If it is different, why might this be? One way of doing this is to ask a colleague to join you on a visit and to give feedback or to observe you on the phone – almost like a direct observation but much more informally. If you have a good relationship with service users you could ask them too, where appropriate.

6.   Use supervision

Discussion with your manager can be really helpful; they should have a view on your EI levels and this will be helpful to you as you begin your new role. You should be able to have a safe and productive discussion around this topic. If your manager knows little about EI then you could help to educate them in this area!

7.   Take it to a team meeting

This is a great topic for discussion at team meetings (and you can claim it as evidence in your ASYE portfolio). All of us are different and have differing levels of skill and abilities in all areas. If you are in a safe and nurturing team this can be a useful exercise, but it should be approached with caution as some colleagues may well find this kind of discussion uncomfortable.

Understanding and using the concept of EI in social work

Tony Morrison (2007) points to the importance of the development of EI skills in social work as being crucial to the effectiveness of the profession and suggests that '*EI is, alongside professional values, one of the cornerstones for effective social work*'. Though there will be many factors that determine the outcome of your case, the relationship or rapport that develops between you as the worker and the service user will be crucial to both the level of engagement you can expect and also in having a positive conclusion to your work. Your levels of EI will clearly play a significant part in this.

Given the above, we are asking you to take what you have learned and apply it to your role as an NQSW. Where to start? Well, a lot of what we have talked about has been to encourage you to look at yourself and to make an analysis (or assessment) of where you are at. Isn't this what we are doing all the time as social workers, working out where people are at? By now you should have a pretty good idea of what EI is and where you are on the scale above – but how does this relate to work and to service users?

One way you can link this knowledge to your work with service users is to think about where they might be and what impact this is having on their current situation. Quite often we do this as we go along but may not have thought about it in this context; it is a new angle from which you may see new and different things in your casework. Think about some of your service users and their levels of EI – a person who abuses another can be said to not have the ability to *value others* or to *accept others* or to *engage in trusting relationships*. This is directly related to the person's levels of EI. How does a parent with low levels of EI build positive EI in their child and how might you help with this?

ACTIVITY · ASSESSING EI IN SERVICE USERS

Using the information in this chapter and other knowledge you may have gained from reading or discussions, think about the following situations and what this tells you about the person's level of EI:

- o a mother who stays with a violent partner when faced with losing her children;
- o a sister who financially abuses an older person with dementia;
- o a father who denies his learning disabled son a place at the local youth club.

How do you think that you as an NQSW can use what you have learned to gain a greater understanding of these situations and provide a quality service for those concerned?

Another way we can link this chapter to our work is by thinking about our own levels of EI and areas we need to develop and to think about how any of this may help our work with service users. For example, how you approach a situation or person will undoubtedly impact on your relationship with them and potentially on the outcome of the case. What happens when you cannot *accept* a person's behaviour? How do you respond to this?

Case Study – Missing the message?

Saj has been qualified for three years and works in an adult team with people with learning difficulties. He completes assessments of need on a regular basis but often has to tell carers that they are ineligible for services. On a number of occasions people have become angry or upset with him and accused him of being insensitive. Saj was concerned about this and discussed this with his manager in supervision as he felt that he might have the wrong approach in his work. He and his manager spent time discussing these incidents and examining what was said and done by both parties and Saj was able to recognise that he was not allowing carers to express their views adequately during the assessment and was not valuing the contribution that the carers were making to the conversation – it appears that he was more driven by the process and getting to the end of the assessment than listening to the frustration of the carers during the process. Saj was not interpreting the other person's feelings correctly so he was unable to use this to inform his responses and to then manage his own behaviour and ultimately respond appropriately to the other person's need. Saj was pleased to have brought this to supervision and was helped to reflect on his practice, which allowed him to make some changes; this resulted in a more positive response to him from the carers.

Don't forget about professional relationships here either. Colleagues' levels of EI will also have an impact upon others – service users, those within the team and others in multidisciplinary working. Watch your colleagues' behaviour and how they express themselves and you will be able to make a good guess about where they need to develop their own EI skills. Or there may be someone who you particularly admire – watch and learn from them.

A WORD ABOUT STRESS

Stress occurs when we feel that things are out of our control and this begins to impact upon our lives in a negative way; when this happens we can move towards emotional overload and our perceptions can soon become distorted as we see things in a negative light – which is the opposite to what we should be aiming for and we know that this can affect us physically and emotionally. When we are aware of our emotions and have well-developed EI skills, stress should become much easier to manage – we can become more resilient. For example, having an 'acceptance of ourselves and others' means that we are less likely to become frustrated by others' inability to engage with a plan or with services; if we remain 'open' to other possibilities, we will not become fixed on one idea and be able to practise more flexibly. Understanding this link will also allow you to accept that sometimes people who use our services do not have highly developed EI skills and this will affect their abilities to engage and to change and that this can lead them to present in a very challenging manner.

As a social worker you may be dealing with people who are in desperately difficult situations and this often causes people to become agitated and stressed, including you as the worker. It is worth taking some time to think about how this will impact upon people's responses and how you can use your knowledge of EI to be a more effective practitioner. You may find yourself in a volatile situation from time to time, but having an understanding of EI will help you to manage this in a more positive way for all concerned; developing your EI skills will enable you to become a more effective worker in these circumstances. Together with other subjects we have covered – stress and burnout and work–life balance, this will allow you to develop into a practitioner who is ready for the challenges of the job. Experience will help, but going into the job as an NQSW having learned about how to look after yourself will give you a head start in any kind of situation.

RESILIENCE

Emotional resilience is closely related to EI. Your emotional resilience can be described as your ability to manage both regular and occasional excessive pressure and the demands placed upon you in life, and to positively adapt to any risk to which you may be exposed. People who are thought more resilient:

- are optimistic and cheerful;
- have a positive life view;
- have good problem-solving skills;
- have good self-esteem;
- are more open to change;
- relish new experiences;
- have a well-developed social support network.

Resilience is thought to be acquired through our early development and secure attachments and further as we experience and overcome difficult situations and stressors within our lives (Howe, 2008).

We have already highlighted that social work is a very rewarding but stressful and demanding job (Rose, 2003) and social workers need to develop resilience to protect their own mental health and well-being, in order to carry out the functions of their role and to provide quality services to service users. The Laming Report (Laming, 2009) noted that *'social workers need to develop "emotional resilience" to manage the challenges from potentially difficult families'* (p 52). This was echoed by the Social Work Task Force (Department of Health, 2009) stating that social work calls for a particular mix of analytical skills, insight, common sense, confidence, resilience, empathy and use of authority but that there is acute concern that a minority of those accepted onto courses have *'difficulty in analysing and conceptualising, and that they lack the maturity, resilience or life experience that con-tribute to becoming a good social worker'* (pp 17–18, paras 1.13 and 1.14). Evidently, EI and resilience are now key components in social work.

As part of developing our EI it is important to consider our resilience (and empathy). Being resilient allows us to cope with stress more effectively. When we are unable to reduce our stress we are not able to read our own needs and feelings, or able to communicate our needs or those of our service users (Hackett and Tebow, 2012). Reflective practice, which we will discuss in Chapter 9, allows you as a social worker not only to look on the surface at your interactions with your service users but also to dig deeper and address the emotional and physical demands of social work upon your own emotional well-being. It is important to ensure that while you may empathise with your service users you must not take on their stress or you risk becoming overloaded (Howe, 2008). You must learn how to deal with these issues positively (as discussed in Chapter 8), and unload the emotional aspects of social work. This will enable you to protect yourself, build up your resilience and do the best job that you can.

Your new habits

You should now have gained a greater understanding of yourself and know more about your own levels of EI and how these affect you and those around you. Take a few minutes and make a list of the things that you will do to improve your levels of EI and how you will ensure that your practice is improved.

Your Toolkit – Now that you have worked through the chapter, consider – how does what you have learned alter your thinking? Record examples of how your EI has affected your day-to-day practice and what impact this has had on your service users and colleagues. Add this to your evidence log.

TAKING IT FURTHER

Howe, D (2008) The Emotionally Intelligent Social Worker. Basingstoke: Palgrave

Matzke, D (2012) Emotional Intelligence in a Nutshell – Personality Patterns for Personal Effectiveness. CreateSpace, Kindle Edition

Websites:

www.mindtools.com/pages/article/newCDV_59.htm

www.unh.edu/emotional_intelligence

6 Practicalities of managing your workload

INTRODUCTION

Becoming a social worker can be an exciting prospect – starting a new role and being given a caseload can be quite daunting. There are a number of demands on your time including learning all about the real world of social work, the day-to-day office workings, putting all that you have learned into practice and remembering the theory which underpins your work. This chapter will help you to decide how best to manage your time and enable you to become an effective practitioner.

- o   Time management (SMART working)
- o   Traffic lights (prioritising)
- o   Dealing with difficult tasks
- o   Diaries and planning
- o   Chairing a meeting
- o   Home visits
- o   Completing large pieces of work
- o   Pause and reflect
- o   Top tips

Links to:

PCF 1 – Professionalism

PCF 5 – Knowledge

PCF 7 – Intervention and Skills

PCF 8 – Contexts and Organisations

TIME MANAGEMENT (SMART WORKING)

The reality for many social workers is that as workloads increase and staffing levels are reduced, learning how to manage our time is becoming an ever more essential skill. As a social worker you will need to develop time management skills in order to keep your work levels under control and to help minimise your stress.

You need to work 'SMART' by identifying the highest priority jobs for your daily and weekly situation. This will help you to stay focused and to work more effectively. SMART working enables us to keep moving towards our goals and objectives (your jobs on your 'task list'). We need to think in terms of these being **S**pecific, **M**easurable, **A**chievable, **R**ealistic and **T**imely.

Working in this way is not only useful in time management but can be utilised in a number of aspects of social work, for example, when setting goals and objectives for your service users. We can also use SMART objectives particularly around risk management (Taylor, 2010, pp 132–3). For example, identify those cases that have the potential to impact most upon those who are more vulnerable and at risk of significant harm. Risk can vary depending upon the different variables and complexities involved in each case and the likelihood of harm.

Specific

Think about what you want to achieve and be specific. The more specific the objective, the better it will be. Keep it simple and straightforward. Ask the who, what, when and how type questions. Who am I doing this for? What do I have to do? When do I need to have this completed? How am I going to do this?

Measurable

You should have a measure so you know when/if you have achieved the task. It is important to have measures to keep you motivated along the way; they are also visible to track your progress and let you know when you've reached the objective or end of the task.

Achievable

Keep the task achievable and attainable. Your objective should not be too far in the future or it will be difficult to keep motivated and on track. Do not let objectives become unrealistic or else you will become frustrated and demotivated. If in doubt, break the task into smaller pieces.

Realistic

Don't try to do something you are not able to achieve. Realistic does not always mean easy; your task may still be difficult but it must be something that is realistic. You may have to change priorities along the way if you have set tasks that are unrealistic; for example, is it realistic to finish the whole report by the end of the week?

Timely

Think about how long the task will take you; keep it in timescales – when do you need to achieve the task by? Set a deadline but these too need to be realistic and achievable. If you do not set a deadline it is likely that other things will take over and become your priority and you will lose your focus and motivation.

ACTIVITY • MY TO DO LIST

Complete part (a) before you read and complete part (b).

Part (a). You have arrived at work this morning with the following tasks in your 'in tray'. You have ten minutes to consider the 'Task List' below and put them into order of priority, and plan how you will deal with these jobs.

Think about which jobs you must do now and which things can be put off and for how long. Some of these jobs may have been left from a previous day so you must ask yourself if you can leave them any longer.

- You have ten case notes to complete from various visits and telephone calls.
- Attend a planning meeting.
- Return a telephone call to a professional following a meeting yesterday.
- Complete a Safeguarding Plan.
- Deal with overdue filing.
- Attend a joint visit with a colleague – this is a two-person visit due to safety.
- Arrange supervision with your manager.
- Arrange a visit to a service user.
- Reply to emails.
- Write a set of minutes from a Safeguarding meeting you chaired two days ago.

Part (b). You have just put your list into order when you receive a telephone call. The colleague with whom you were to undertake your joint visit has phoned in sick. You must attend the meeting and this is a two-person visit due to safety issues. Also, your manager has just said they need half an hour to update you on a new case that you will be allocated later today.

Do you need to rearrange your list and reprioritise it? If so, you have a further five minutes to do this.

At the end of the activity, think about how you went about planning your day, how did you feel about it, what factors influenced your planning, were you happy with the outcome?

TRAFFIC LIGHTS

Using the list in the above activity, look again.

Mark all PRIORITY jobs as Red

Mark all IMPORTANT jobs as Amber

Mark all ESSENTIAL jobs as Green

You should give yourself a timescale for each traffic light; eg, all red – to do today; all amber – to do tomorrow; all green – to do by day three. You may not always have any red or amber jobs, although you may have several greens on your list which are or may become a red or amber if something happens, ie, a case may become a safeguarding issue and therefore may become a red. Your list is not static.

If you don't want to use traffic lights, use numbers or invent your own system, but remember the importance of the job at hand!

You can decide which tasks you can do in order of priority/importance, etc. It is recommended that you do not leave items at green for too long as those jobs are still essential and if they are not completed and are put off, the jobs will then become urgent. Jobs can travel back up the traffic light from green to amber to red – social work is about real life; our work changes all the time.

Procrastination

The old saying is true, 'don't put off for tomorrow what can be done today'. 'I'll do it later' is a fatal trap and can lead to your own downfall. Work can pile up and become overwhelming. Procrastinating is something that you do not want to get used to, so try not to develop this bad habit. You never know when you will get an emergency and you will have to renumber your 'to do' list, so putting off jobs for another day should be avoided as you never know what will come up in the world of social work. It is a good idea to think in terms of 'consequences' as this can help to focus your mind – ask yourself: what will the consequences be if I put off this task?

DEALING WITH DIFFICULT TASKS

As a social worker you will have to deal with some difficult tasks. This could be a difficult person or situation or telephone call or meeting with your supervisor, and you may feel unprepared and nervous about this. Often this task can start as a 'green' task but become a 'red' task because you are wary of dealing with it. If you are faced with this situation the first thing to do is acknowledge your feelings – it is OK to feel like this and though it will lessen with experience, be assured that experienced social workers can face this kind of situation.

ACTIVITY • MY DIFFICULT SITUATION

Think about a task you have to complete that you feel is really difficult; this may be a phone call or a visit or giving someone bad news. Think through why you might be feeling this way and find someone to talk this through with. Think through your options and list them, writing down all possible outcomes and responses. From this make a plan of action and if necessary role play the plan with a colleague or supervisor. This will help you to feel more confident. Once you have your plan, carry it out as soon as you can and afterwards use critical reflection to help you to examine how things went.

Sometimes these situations will arise suddenly and without warning but the more you plan and face situations head on, the more prepared you will become. The next situation will not seem so daunting and your reflection will ensure that you will have learned a lot and developed both personally and professionally. Think of these situations in terms of a challenge and congratulate yourself on your successes.

DIARIES AND PLANNING

Time management is not just about keeping your diary in good order – though with both traditional paper diaries and electronic diaries now in use, you may have to rethink the way your appointments are booked. Who else may have access to your diary? Do they book appointments for you? Do they also have access to your paper diary? Do you need two different methods? What other information is in your diary/how else can your diary be useful to you?

When you are requesting information from another professional or a colleague, set a deadline and inform them when you want the information or report; otherwise it will not become a priority for them. A good tip is not to give them the last day of your own deadline, give yourself a few days grace so that you can have time to complete your report once you have their information. You need to keep track of what information or reports you are waiting for as you may be waiting for several things at the same time. Add these things to a list or into your diary.

Case Study – Making the most of technology

While writing this book, we initially planned to meet up every couple of weeks in order to plan and discuss our work, and who would do what, etc. We live two and a half hours away from one another, therefore these meetings would have to be carefully planned and scheduled to fit in with our own working commitments and busy home lives. One Saturday we had planned to meet in a central location, both travelling over an hour to the venue. However, one author already has a commitment to driving 500 miles per week to work and back, had done additional driving that week to visit a sick relative in hospital and had been unwell herself. The other author had had a hectic schedule that week and had some additional work to do at home to get an assignment completed for an urgent deadline. This meeting, however, was very important and needed to be completed. After some discussion about where to meet, venue, time to travel to the venue we decided to try the meeting using Skype.

This worked really well. It was free and saved time, money and energy. We were able to complete our meeting using Skype in the time that it would have taken us just to reach the venue, and that's without the return journey. Following this we had regular meetings using Skype and with regular emails, we only met face to face when we really had to do so.

Think about ways you can save time in this way and make technology work for you.

Planning time when you can have minimal interruptions is often key to success. You may work in a hot desking situation or in an open plan office, which can make life very difficult when planning your work. You may need to think about booking a quiet space if this is not readily available. Try to delegate any work that you can, get someone to take your phone calls or put your phone (even the mobile) on answer phone. When trying to meet an important deadline, and unless you are 'on duty' or awaiting an urgent call, don't make yourself too accessible all the time, otherwise people will think you should always be available to speak to them. If you answer that call it is likely that you will get distracted. When you do have to take or make a phone call, make sure you tell your caller you are sorry but you only have five minutes so you need to be brief. In the same way you can plan meetings and visits (see below). Try to plan your call with objectives and the information that you need to convey; it is a good idea to make a brief list of these.

Emails

Emails are a part of our everyday working life. Checking and reading our mail can become very time-consuming and take up a lot of our working day, especially when we begin to check our inbox every couple of minutes. A good tip is to turn off your email 'pop up' so that when you are typing on your computer you are not interrupted or distracted by a 'pop up' informing you that you have mail as no doubt you will be tempted to have a look at your message.

Remember, do not send unnecessary emails. When you do look in your inbox, try to deal with any emails immediately and then either archive or delete them. Don't leave mail unnecessarily in your inbox as this becomes another time-consuming job at a later date when you have to sort them out. Keep your emails concise and straight to the point; don't use them for complex issues. Ensure that you deal effectively with spam mail; most works computers will ensure the correct settings are in place so that you don't receive it.

Writing lists

When you go to the supermarket for your weekly groceries it is much easier when you have prepared a list. You can go down your list and only put in your trolley the things that are on the list. This is quicker and often cheaper than a random shop. You also come home with things you actually want. You can adopt this idea within your working day.

For example, when you are attending a visit or a meeting and something comes up that you wish to discuss with your manager, perhaps in supervision, add it to your list of things to discuss – your supervision agenda. This helps with your preparation for your supervision and as an added bonus, your manager thinks 'yes, they have given this idea some thought'.

Once you have written these things on your list you can then forget about them until your meeting or discussion.

CHAIRING A MEETING

Meetings are a major part of the job of a social worker. You may be responsible for chairing your own meetings, eg Core Group meetings, Care Programme Approach (CPA) or planning meetings. It goes without saying that you should not have a meeting just for the sake of meeting up – death by meetings. Think of other ways you can share information. If you do have to meet up, there are lots of things to consider prior to the meeting which will save you time and effort and ensure you use your time more effectively. If you can delegate tasks to your admin/business support colleagues delegate, delegate … however, if you have to do this yourself you need to consider the following points.

Before the meeting

Type	What is the purpose of the meeting? What do you want to achieve?
Venue	This needs to be accessible and comfortable, consider layout of room, drinks, visual aids, who will meet and greet, who sits where?
Time	Choose a time to suit as many people as possible, definitely the most important people – the service user.
Disabilities	Does anyone have a disability – are there any special considerations for your service user or colleagues that you have to consider? Are they attending, do they need help preparing?
Agenda	Develop an agenda with your key members and service user and distribute it before the meeting.
Reports	Prepare and share any reports in good time.

At the meeting

It is OK to be nervous. Chairing a meeting is a skill that you will develop over time and you will find your own way – watch others and see if their style suits you; you will pick up some good tips by doing this.

You must be an 'active listener'. Have an agenda, and prioritise this with the group, keeping an approximate time for your agenda items. Start and end the meeting on time. Keep your eye on the clock and indicate the approximate end time of the meeting. It is important as the chair of the meeting to ensure that everyone gets time to discuss each issue but that you keep control. If people cannot agree or your discussion is going around in a circle, you may have to be assertive and end the discussion. You could suggest that the meeting notes that this aspect of the discussion was not resolved and suggest that this subject requires further discussion outside of the meeting or at another time. You must keep focused on what is being said and by whom and what decisions are being made. Make notes of these key decisions, action points and future plans, for example, when making Child in Need Plans or Pathway Plans. Ensure that your service users, if present, have time to express their wishes and feelings or their advocate has time to do this on their behalf. Plan to allow time for this.

ACTIVITY • PLANNING A MEETING

Imagine you are going to chair a planning meeting. Make a list of all the things to consider in terms of the venue, other professionals, service users, timings, and admin tasks. Also consider yourself and your own thoughts and feelings – is there anything that you are unsure of? Include the aims of the meeting, potential difficulties that may arise and tasks that may be agreed.

Once you have made your list, you can use this as a basis for your future work. It is a good idea to make up a proforma, which you can print off and use as a checklist for future meetings.

In a similar way, you can use a proforma for planning home visits (see below).

After the meeting

Use critical reflection to help you to improve managing your meetings and discuss any issues in supervision or with colleagues.

HOME VISITS

In times of austerity it is likely your manager is asking you to cut down on all unnecessary mileage and visits; you must ask yourself ... is my visit absolutely necessary? Obviously social workers have to see service users for many reasons.

Home visits are vital to your work and you can gain crucial information from even the shortest time in a person's home. Think about what you want from your visit. Outline three to five objectives and you will find it easier to achieve your outcomes and return to the office with the appropriate information you need from your visit. Consider the care plan, the current situation and think SMART.

Allocate a time to the visit, bearing in mind the travel. Can you visit anyone else in that area? Plan your diary around geographical areas if it is possible. This is particularly important for both time planning and cost of fuel.

COMPLETING LARGE PIECES OF WORK

When undertaking a project or a complex piece of work (maybe a court report), it is often a good idea to devise a plan of work. Time spent thinking about your project in 'chunks' will save time in the long run. Plot your tasks so that you can plan the time you need to complete the work. Be realistic. Use the SMART objectives mentioned earlier.

A Gantt chart is a very common and effective way of displaying a breakdown of your schedule to help you implement your activities/tasks. The Gantt chart will determine the minimum time required for the project. You could use a Gantt chart prior to completing a social care single assessment, where you have a strict deadline of a maximum of 45 working days to complete. You can break up chunks of time into days or weeks to help you break down the tasks, ie, visits to schools, home visits to see parents, talking to the child(ren), time for writing up the report, sharing the report with the family. This will help you keep a track of what you need to do.

Gantt charts can be simple or sophisticated depending on your task. You can decide how detailed you want your chart to be and how much information you want to put in it. The one shown below is a very basic Gantt chart but did the job.

 ## Case Study – Gantt chart

A Practice Supervisor in a hospital social work team was charged with the job of 'redesigning' the 'Referral Form' for all referrals to the hospital social work teams. There were four hospitals of which two were main Accident and Emergency hospitals and two were non-accident hospitals. Referrals to the hospital social work teams were received from the hospital wards. The social work teams were Local Authority Adult Social Care Teams and the hospitals were under part of the NHS Trust.

This task was completed over a period of 19 weeks. In order to complete the project a Gantt chart was used to show a breakdown of the project into manageable portions and to help plan a realistic timescale for completing the task.

The chart is just a guide and things can be switched as you go along, particularly as things may go wrong and schedules have to change.

See Gantt chart.

Activity	Week number								
	1–2	3–4	5–6	7–8	9–10	11–12	13–14	16–17	18–19
Arrange meeting with team managers to discuss form (×4)	▓								
Discuss form with selected wards (W7, W1, W9)	▓	▓							
Meet with team managers									
Hospital 1		▓							
Hospital 2					▓				
Hospital 3						▓			
Discussion with Hospital 4			▓						
Meet with Business Support				▓					
Prepare draft referral form				▓					
Book slot at hospital review meeting		▓							
Meet (or talk) with Business Modernisation Manager		▓(T)			▓(T) (M)▓				
Prepare draft referral form				▓					
Present to hospital review meeting					▓				

Continued overleaf

Activity	Week number								
	1–2	3–4	5–6	7–8	9–10	11–12	13–14	16–17	18–19
Make any alterations and send for approval						▪			
Discuss with Matron, Ward 7a re trial						⌐			
Trial form						▪	▪		
Collate feed-back from Ward 7a							▪		
Any final alterations following feed-back/Discuss with Senior Manager							▪		
Send form to Modernisation Manager for numbering								▪	
Roll out form across each hospital								▪	▪
Form available for download-ing for use by staff									▪

PAUSE AND REFLECT

You will recall that as a student, or as an NQSW on your ASYE journey, that a great deal of emphasis is put on your reflective journal and how important this is. Allowing yourself time to pause and reflect upon the actions and decisions you have made during your day (or week) is very important. Try and continue to find this time to think about what you have completed, how effective your action was and if you could do anything differently next time (this is discussed in more detail in Chapter 9). This is important regardless of what position you hold within the organisation. Try to diarise time for this.

It is important to understand where you are in the development of your knowledge and skill. To try to make sense of this, Noel Burch developed the 'conscious competence' theory in the 1970s. Originally this theory identified four stages of learning.

As an NQSW you will be at the first stage of development or 'unconscious incompetence' when you do not understand how to do something or that you have not yet developed the knowledge and skill required for a particular task. You may not recognise the task that needs completing. Once you understand the task, in stage two, 'conscious incompetence', you are still unable to complete the task but acknowledge that this is the case and see that there must be a solution. In the 'conscious competence' stage (stage three), you will become aware of how to do the task but you have to concentrate hard in order to complete the task to a competent standard and have a 'conscious' involvement in the learning and completion of the task. Finally you reach stage four, 'unconscious competence'. You have been doing the job for a while and have become very competent; perhaps you are doing it 'without thinking' about it and you could teach someone else to do it (http://en.wikipedia.org/wiki/Four_stages_of_ competence).

Since this four-stage theory was developed, there has been a fifth stage added, and perhaps this is the reason why we need to give time to 'pause and reflect' regularly to be sure that we do not fall victim to this fifth stage, 'conscious competence of unconscious competence', in other words becoming complacent in what we do.

ACTIVITY · WHERE AM I AT?

Think of two tasks that you complete each day, one a newly acquired skill (perhaps a work-related task that is new to you) and one that you learned a while ago (this may be driving or some other practical skill). Apply the above theory to each of them and think about what stage you are at and how you moved through the different developmental stages.

Once you have completed this activity continue, and consider whether you are in stage five (below) with any of your activities.

This chapter has given you information and activities on managing your time. There is more information available online and there are many books available on the subject. This is crucial to your success as a social worker. You CAN manage your time effectively if you are organised and plan ahead. (Remember the habits you form now are the ones you will keep.)

OUR TOP TIPS FOR TIME MANAGEMENT

- Use your diary effectively.
- Plan your day and week ahead, leave gaps between appointments.
- Cluster visits that are in the same area.
- Do not over-commit yourself.
- Diary in thinking and planning time.
- Leave time for unexpected events.

- Never plan to complete reports by 'the last minute'.
- Always take at least half an hour for lunch, away from your desk.
- Learn to say 'No'.
- Book some time with 'no phone calls'.
- Set aside time to check emails.
- Break down large tasks into small chunks.
- Use a 'to do' list.
- Plan to do at least one 'difficult' task at the start of each day.
- Think SMART.
- Take time to pause and reflect.
- Take a computer break at least once in an hour – make tea for everyone!
- Keep your desk and surroundings clean and tidy.

Your new habits

This chapter has lots of handy hints and tips for managing your time. What have you learned that you will take forward into your working life? You could write a note in your diary to remind you to keep to your favourite new habits.

 Your Toolkit – Now that you have worked through the chapter on managing your workload, and completed the activities suggested, turn to the Toolkit and fill in the sections that you feel are appropriate. Remember, many sections will overlap and the more you put into the Toolkit, the more you will get out of it.

 TAKING IT FURTHER

Atkins, B (2013) Personal Safety for Social Workers and Health Professionals. Northwich: Critical Publishing

Evans, C (2008) Time Management for Dummies (UK edition). Chichester: John Wiley & Sons

Forster, M (2006) Do It Tomorrow and Other Secrets of Time Management. London: Hodder & Stoughton

Websites:

www.mindtools.com

How you can manage stress and avoid burnout

INTRODUCTION

In this chapter we will discuss stress and burnout, and explore how this can impact upon social workers. We will also help you to build resilience in this area by recognising signs and symptoms and by encouraging you to develop your own strategies and coping mechanisms. Burnout is addressed and the quiz will help you to see where you might be on the burnout scale. Other activities are included throughout the chapter and there is also a brief look at organisational change and its effect upon workers.

The authors are not medical practitioners. If you are concerned that you are experiencing any of the warning signs of stress or burnout, you should see a doctor for a health check. Your doctor can help you determine whether or not your symptoms are stress-related as the signs and symptoms of stress can be caused by other health-related problems and it is important to get yourself checked out. Most of all don't panic – there is plenty you can do to get back on track.

o   Social work(ers) and stress – research
o   Understanding stress
o   Burnout
o   Burnout – signs and symptoms
o   Coping with change – the change/coping cycle
o   What can we do about it?
o   Burnout/stress management techniques

Links to:

PCF 1 – Professionalism

PCF 2 – Values and Ethics

PCF 5 – Knowledge

PCF 7 – Intervention and Skills

PCF 8 – Contexts and Organisations

SOCIAL WORK(ERS) AND STRESS

Let's look at the research.

As you will be aware, the media is very quick to present social work in a negative light. However, it is important to put this into perspective and we will look at both sides of the coin and balance out this view. There are a great number of positive elements to social work and it is heartening to see newly qualified workers come into social work with positive and refreshing attitudes and sparkle.

You will no doubt be able to recall the tragedies that social workers in all sectors have to deal with from child deaths, abuse of vulnerable adults, to older people living isolated and alone in squalor. In the UK, a number of Serious Case Reviews within social work and social care have historically highlighted systemic failures with social care systems, structures and organisations, evidencing the failures within the very organisations in which we work and arguing that we should protect people from significant harm. Munro (2011a) criticises the organisational bureaucracies, targets, complex IT systems and timescales that social workers have to contend with, which all add to the stress upon the social worker and lead to them being less effective and less able to safeguard service users.

Social work is considered to be a very stressful occupation with the social worker having to contend with and balance many factors such as low morale, difficulty in the recruitment and retention of social workers, high workloads, the needs of the organisation, including 'reshaping' and change (particularly within the current economic climate), lack of recognition, service user advocacy and bureaucracy.

Despite this, however, and before you despair and worry you've chosen the wrong profession, Collins (2007) emphasises there are factors that enable social workers to persist and continue with their work such as resilience, optimism and personal and peer group support which contribute to the positive well-being of social workers. Rose (2003) stated that social work is among the most rewarding jobs. Social workers obtain high satisfaction working with service users and they are also committed to making a difference to people's lives and are highly motivated (Eborall and Garmeson, 2001; Huxley et al., 2005). This is why many of us choose to enter social work. Coffey et al.'s (2004) study noted that 4.1 per cent of salaried staff were off sick with stress-related illness, but did not highlight the fact that 95.9 per cent were well and present at work. Rose (2003) highlights the point that social work sits within the top 20 groups that enjoy high job satisfaction and social workers have a high level of commitment. If you ask your colleagues they will agree they enjoy the challenge of the job, variety of task, teamwork and multidisciplinary work and autonomy within their roles.

Social work practice is an exciting and challenging career with 'change' being a pivotal part of the social work role and the profession itself. Recent years have seen the transfer of regulation to the Health and Care Professions Council, the development of the Professional Capabilities Framework giving social workers at ALL levels capability statements to help identify and strengthen their continued professional development and the Assessed and Supported Year in Employment. These changes have enhanced social work, and make this a great profession to be a part of. With such change however, comes uncertainty for some, and this in itself may lead to some workers becoming increasingly stressed in the short term at the perception that too much happens too quickly. The advantage for you is that this is all new to you as a student or an NQSW and you will be in it from the beginning with no preconceived ideas or expectations of 'how it used to be'.

Collins et al.'s (2010) study on stress in social work students highlighted that they enjoyed a high sense of personal achievement and accomplishment. Although there was recognition that some experience low self-esteem and emotional exhaustion, it was suggested they would benefit from mutual group support, tutorial support and stress management courses. Many also have additional stress balancing full-time study and paid work, which is something you will perhaps be able to relate to.

ACTIVITY · STRESS AT WORK

People perceive situations differently and this includes how we interpret and manage our stress both at work and at home. Our personalities and our behaviour frame how we manage different stressors with factors such as our perception, motivation and attitude.

How do you currently manage your stress at work?

Take 5–10 minutes to carefully think about this question and list your answers. Think about the different situations you are in at the time you become stressed and the triggers. Then think about how you deal with the different situations. (You can do this exercise separately for your home life but here we concentrate on your stress at work.)

Give yourself a number for your stress levels.

On a scale of 1 to 10 what is YOUR number?

0 – – – – – – | – – – – – – | – – – – – – | – – – – – – 10

No stress at all   Highly stressed

Stress at work can be caused by both 'overload' and 'underload', ie, simply by being bored, not having enough to do and not being stimulated or challenged by your work. As an NQSW you will have many new and exciting challenges to keep you interested for years to come in your career. Stress is also caused when you experience 'role confusion' – this is brought about when you are not sure about what you have to do in your job. To avoid this, don't be afraid to ask your manager to clarify things to ensure both you and your supervisor are clear about exactly what you are doing, and why. It is much better to ask at the beginning than have to do something again or to make a mistake, particularly as you are making decisions that affect people's lives. When you are unsure of your role and what is expected of you, the pressure and stress can become too much. Stress and panic then occurs and this impacts upon your health and well-being and your overall confidence, and thus the confidence others have in you.

UNDERSTANDING STRESS

Stress can be caused through many different things in your life such as financial pressure, home life and relationships. Stress can also be caused by pressures at work. Stress may be caused by having to balance all these different factors rather than one specific thing that is happening in your life.

The NHS simply states that stress is the feeling of being under too much mental or emotional pressure and that when things become too much and you are unable to cope, this is when the pressure turns into stress (see www.nhs.uk/Conditions/stress-anxiety-depression/Pages/understanding-stress.aspx).

The Health and Safety Executive (HSE) states:

> **Work-related stress, depression or anxiety is defined as a harmful reaction people have to undue pressures and demands placed on them at work**
>
> (HSE, 2016, p 2)

The Health & Safety Executive's Labour Force Survey (LFS) 2015/16 show:

> **The total number of working days lost due to this condition in 2015/16 was 11.7 million days. This equated to an average of 23.9 days lost per case.**
>
> **In 2015/16 stress accounted for 37% of all work related ill health cases and 45% of all working days lost due to ill health.**
>
> **Stress is more prevalent in public service industries, such as education; health and social care; and public administration and defence.**
>
> **By occupation, jobs that are common across public service industries (such as healthcare workers; teaching professionals; business, media and public service professionals) show higher levels of stress as compared to all jobs.**
>
> (Cited in HSE Nov 16 p 2 www.hse.gov.uk/Statistics/causdis/stress/index.htm)

Stress can come from the external environment but it can also be self-generated, by worrying about things that are often out of our control – 'internal stress'.

We have a typical 'innate' response to stress known as 'fight or flight'. This automatic reaction helps us deal with danger and act quickly in stressful situations. When you perceive a threat, your nervous system responds by releasing stress hormones. You will no doubt have felt your body respond to this when your heart beats faster, your breathing is accelerated and you start to sweat. Your body reacts in this way to protect you and heighten your senses. Long-term exposure to too much stress can be detrimental to your physical health and well-being. Stress can leave you more susceptible to anxiety and depression (Stranks, 2005; Thompson et al., 1994; Williams and Cooper, 2002).

Having said this, however, don't be afraid of having some stress in your life. We all experience stress and some of this is positive; it keeps us going and motivated looking forward to exciting new challenges. It's all about staying in control of your stress and building up tolerance and support and having a good work–life balance.

ACTIVITY · STRESS AND YOUR SIGNS AND SYMPTOMS

Before you continue, and having just read the text about the effects of stress, using the headings below, take five minutes to write down any signs and symptoms you may have experienced.

Cognitive   **Emotional**   **Behavioural**   **Physical**

Now compare them to the list below of the most common signs and symptoms of stress.

STRESS SIGNS AND SYMPTOMS

Cognitive

Mood swings
Poor judgement
Poor concentration
Seeing only the negative
Anxious or racing thoughts
Constantly worrying
Deterioration in memory

Emotional

Breakdown of relationships
Irritable or short-tempered
Getting agitated, difficulty relaxing
Feeling overwhelmed
Sense of loneliness and isolation
Depressed or very unhappy
Lack of self-worth/esteem

Behavioural

Eating too much or too little
Sleeping too much or too little
Cutting yourself off from friends
Procrastinating/neglecting things
Alcohol or drug misuse
Increase in smoking
Nervous habits (nail biting, pacing)

Physical

Aches and pains – eg backache
Diarrhoea or constipation
Nausea, dizziness, light-headedness
Chest pain, rapid heartbeat
Loss of libido
Frequent colds
Muscle tension (neck/back pain)

BURNOUT

Collings and Murray (1996) state that burnout is a serious feature of chronic stress and can impair the human service worker's effectiveness, resulting in a high turnover of staff.

Burnout is a state of physical, emotional and mental exhaustion. Having burnout is a deeper, more overwhelming state than stress. Burnout is when there are too many demands and these are constant. A person with burnout is 'empty' and they have an inability to feel sympathy and empathy for others, losing sensitivity to personal emotions. Burnout causes physical and mental disorders and a person may have chronic tiredness, cognitive dysfunction, sleep disorders and can develop depression with physical symptoms which may include cardiovascular and other serious problems.

A person with stress

They arrive at work to a full 'in tray' but someone suffering with stress will usually get through this work and have a sense of hope. They may say something like:

I'll be fine, if I can just get through this pile of work, things will be OK.

A person with burnout

They will feel hopeless, lonely and would not be able to contemplate even attempting the 'in tray'; they can't see the light at the end of the tunnel. That feeling of hope of their situation ever changing for the better has gone. They lose trust in life and things seem senseless and aimless.

How a person perceives stress and the issues causing the stress and what action they take will impact upon whether or not a person reaches burnout. It may only take a few stressors for one person to reach burnout whereas another person may have multiple stressors and not reach burnout. Other factors suggesting a susceptibility to burnout include:

- age;
- difficulty communicating with others;
- an inability to express one's feelings in words;
- being a workaholic;
- already experiencing a high level of stress.

Masson and Morrison (1991) discuss the issue of social workers who are on 'duty' and who are faced with unpredictability, uncertainty and rising anxiety levels, being constantly in a state of readiness for new referrals and prepared for anything and everything that the day can bring – however difficult and challenging. This can have a significant impact upon social workers as it is a highly reactive situation with unknown demands. As an NQSW you may want to consider this if you are working in a 'duty' team. Are you ready for this?

Emotional exhaustion is the basic factor behind professional burnout. This is characterised by lack of energy for each new day and having emotional overstrain. You may well develop low self-esteem; this is the inner side of emotional exhaustion. You begin to 'depersonalise' your service users. They no longer appear as real people and they are just seen as part of your job and your daily routine. A person with burnout will avoid service users and colleagues and be both 'physically' and 'emotionally' distant. You do not see others' situations as real or empathise with them as you would normally do. You find yourself distancing and avoiding situations where you have to mix with colleagues, peers and friends and you become flat, unable to be responsive and act automatically to things. Burnout can appear in stages until it reaches a chronic stage and in some cases stress and burnout can be fatal (Thompson et al., 1994). Have a look around your team; think about your peers. Can you identify any of these factors in your colleagues?

Your doctor may prescribe anti-depressants but anti-depressants do not tackle the issue of 'causation'. They may, however, allow you to reach a position where you can begin to move forward and deal with the situation. You should always consult your doctor if you feel you are suffering stress or burnout. Being aware of the signs and symptoms of your own vulnerabilities and putting strategies in place to deal with them can help stop you becoming a candidate for stress and burnout.

Organisations can play a large part in reducing stressors within the environment where you work, at a personal level, a team level and an organisational level (Thompson et al., 1994; also see Chapter 8). Many organisations have gone a long way since the recognition of stress and burnout and the need for a good 'work–life balance', and have put policies and procedures in place to aid this. The ASYE should help protect new social workers coming into the workforce. It will allow you time to adjust, giving you the opportunity to explore your vulnerabilities within structured supervision and career routes, and enabling you to develop a firm foundation to build resilience alongside your increasing experience.

BURNOUT – SIGNS AND SYMPTOMS

Behavioural

- Emotional outbursts including crying a lot
- Decrease in workflow activity
- Avoiding and neglecting responsibilities
- Isolating yourself from others – friends and colleagues
- Taking longer to do things you used to have no problem doing
- Using food, drugs or alcohol as a coping mechanism
- Taking out your frustrations on others, short-tempered
- Arriving to work late and/or leaving early
- Increase in phoning in sick, making excuses

Physical

- Feeling tired and exhausted most of the time
- Lowered immunity, feeling sick a lot
- Frequent headaches
- Muscle aches and tension including back/spinal pain
- Increased blood pressure
- Change in appetite – weight loss

- Changes in your sleeping pattern
- Gastroenterological problems

Emotional

- Anger and frustration
- Frequent feelings of anxiety and mood change
- Doubting yourself and thinking you'll only fail
- Feeling helpless, trapped and defeated
- Detachment and feeling alone
- Feeling demotivated – lack of self-esteem
- Negative outlook all the time, being more cynical
- Decreased satisfaction and sense of accomplishment

Not all these symptoms occur simultaneously. The development of burnout is an individual process.

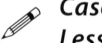

Case Study –
Lessons learned

Majid was an NQSW and began working in a Children's Safeguarding duty team and he really wanted to make a good impression. He spent the first few weeks of his new job busily going from visit to visit, writing up assessments, attending meetings, writing up plans and was co-working a case where the children were brought into Police Protection and ended up living with foster carers. He also got to attend court. He saw that others in the office were all getting on with the job and felt that they were perhaps too busy to help him, so he did not ask when he needed support. In the sixth week his supervision was cancelled by the team manager. Majid carried on and thought he was fine. He was then given a really challenging case which involved a hostile family and domestic violence. By this time Majid was feeling more a part of the team and felt that he was managing OK. He began to fill his diary more and he started to go into the office earlier and finish later, and didn't always take his lunch. At his next supervision his manager asked to look at his diary and this enabled him to 'press the pause button' and discuss what was happening for him. Majid recognised how stress was building up and that he was slowly but surely developing bad habits at this early stage and needed strategies in place to address this. There was a lot of learning here for Majid and since then he has ensured that he regularly discusses issues in supervision and always asks for help when he needs it.

ACTIVITY · BURNOUT QUIZ

Try our quiz to see if you are experiencing burnout

Questions	Never	Rarely	Sometimes	Often	Most of the time
Are you working harder but accomplishing less?					
Do you get lack of recognition at work for the good work you do?					
Are you clear about your job role and what's expected of you?					
Do you feel tired and exhausted more often than you used to?					
Do you forget important things?					
Is your job monotonous and boring?					
Do you feel stimulated and up for the challenge in your job?					
Do you feel disillusioned with things and people around you?					

Continued overleaf

Questions	Never	Rarely	Sometimes	Often	Most of the time
Do you have a view that your glass is always 'half empty'?					
Do you feel you always need to be in control of what's going on?					
Are you trying to be all things to all people?					
Are you waking early or not sleeping very well?					
Are you becoming more irritable?					
Do you have headaches more often than usual?					
Do you suffer from back or muscle pain?					

Now you need to add up your scores. Give yourself points as shown below:

Scores:

Never: 1   Often: 4

Rarely: 2   Most of the time: 5

Sometimes: 3

Continued overleaf

Results:

15–18: You are doing OK, no real signs of any burnout.

19–32: You are still OK, but if some symptoms are severe you need to watch out and look at those particular areas and think about how you can do things differently.

33–49: You're scoring a little high – there is some risk of burnout. Take a look at putting some strategies in place to deal with the areas that are scoring high. Do this as soon as possible – you don't want it to creep up on you.

50–59: You may be at severe risk of burnout – seek advice from your doctor as soon as possible.

60–75: This could become very serious. Make some urgent lifestyle changes – seek help and advice from your doctor.

This is only a guide and you may want to do this test on a different day and time to give you a more balanced view.

COPING WITH CHANGE

Change is something that we experience at different times in our lives. This can be a major contributory factor to stress and burnout. Many statutory organisations have periods of change. They may call this a 'reorganisation', 'restructuring' or 'reshaping'. Many local authorities continue to 'reshape' their departments due to the downturn in the economic climate and cuts to services, although, not all restructures are negative. It is a factor that is often out of our control. Changes may also be in our personal lives such as bereavement or the birth of a child. Change can be a time of immense stress. How we cope with this is very important. Understanding change will hopefully make this process less stressful for you. Within social work, being able to adapt to change is essential for you and to help service users whose lives are often chaotic and full of change. You must remember that when you are faced with, or are managing other people through the *'cycle of change'* there will be times when you, your colleagues or indeed the families you are working with, will relapse. It is important to remember that it is very difficult to sustain change for long periods, espe-cially in the early stages. Those affected will be trying to overcome their own difficulties and their own challenges and will all manage change with a different approach. You must consider that many of the families you deal with may not have the resilience and capacity to overcome change in the same way as yourself and that this can be for a whole host of reasons. For many this process is emotionally demanding and what may seem something and nothing to one person may be a huge mountain for someone else.

Think about a major change in your life and how you and those around you managed this. Look at the cycle below and see if you can identify the stages that you may have gone through.

The change/coping cycle

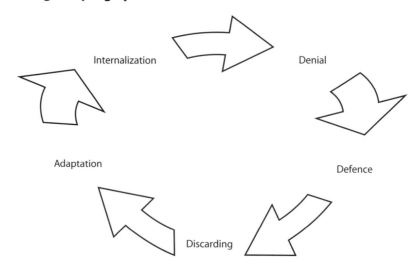

From Carnall (2007, pp 240–4), with permission of Pearson Education Limited.

The five stages

Denial – people deny the need for change and are resistant – 'We have always done things this way, it's OK'.

Defence – the realities of change become clear and people realise that they must under-take new tasks. This can lead to feelings of frustration and depression and in some people may lead to 'defensive' behaviour such as involving trade unions and attending protest marches.

Discarding – people begin to let go of the past and look forward, accepting that change is inevitable and necessary.

Adaptation – mutual adaptation emerges. Individuals begin to test new situations and new ways of working, learning from their own and others' experiences. Teams may start to become more cohesive once again as they start to work out new regimes together.

Internalisation – in the final part, new relationships and ways of working have been tried, modified and accepted. People are aware again of the expectations of self and others. However, some individuals take much longer to achieve this stage, particularly if they have been reluctant to accept the need for these changes at the start of the process.

In all stages of the change/coping cycle both self-esteem and performance are affected in different ways by different people. With organisational change, how you feel about your job and your employer will affect your performance and work activity. The journey through change can bring about a variety of different emotions and outcomes for everyone. Stress, however, is not synonymous with being overworked or experiencing change, it can occur when there is a combination of daily hassles which outweighs a person's capacity to cope; once again these triggers are different for everyone. You may be able to cope more successfully with stress in some aspect of your life than in others. Your coping mechanisms may be different. It is in the organisation's best interest to take effective steps to reduce each employee's overall level of stress, thus improving their workforce and outputs as well as their profitability. This is known as 'discretionary effort' (Carnall, 2007; Grimes, 2005; Williams and Cooper, 2002).

WHAT CAN WE DO ABOUT IT?

It is essential that you build your own personal coping strategies to counter stress and burnout. It is important, also, to remember that your manager has a responsibility to help you manage this too.

Resilient people are seen to be cheerful, optimistic and energetic in their approach to life, welcoming new experiences and being emotionally positive (Howe, 2008). Do you recognise these positive features in yourself? Those who are resilient face similar problems and stresses and do experience negative emotions but these are offset with positive feelings; therefore they are not overwhelmed. Collins (2008) suggests that resilient social workers, when faced with negative and unpleasant experiences within their work such as traumatic events, discrimination, deprivation and resource implications, are able to bounce back and learn from their experience. Howe (2008) believes that emotionally intelligent social workers understand the anger and anxiety experienced by their service users, leading to the successful understanding of the origins of these feelings and how to manage them. The emotionally intelligent social worker has to be aware of their own stress and feelings towards the service users and their defences. As a social worker, when you find a successful resolution to a stressful situation, you should encounter happiness and pride. If you are unable to regulate the stress that service users unload onto you during a visit, this can take its toll on your emotional well-being. This is known as vicarious trauma.

Vicarious trauma happens over time and is a cumulative effect on people working with survivors who have had difficult and significant life experiences. It occurs as a result of witnessing or hearing about other people's suffering. As you empathise with the other person you feel their pain and you can experience some of what they have experienced. You may feel some of that person's grief, anger and fear. Some workers feel responsible for the person who has suffered the harm and you become overwhelmed and have a sense of burden and hopelessness and this impacts upon your own well-being. Over time this process can lead to changes in your psychological, physical and spiritual well-being (www.headington-institute.org/files/vtmoduletemplate2_ready_v2_85791.pdf).

As you develop skills and knowledge you will be able to use the negative emotions of service users to allow them to reflect and move forward but first you need to be able to regulate your emotions and stress levels.

Think about how you may use the following:

Support network – a strong support network of colleagues, peers, family and friends. This is in addition to management support. Team meetings help share the load and discuss uncertainties within the team. They help build morale and share information with employees, share decision making and clarify role conflict and ambiguity.

Supervision – regular supervision from your line manager is essential. Supervision should improve morale, reduce the stress impinging on the social worker and allow shared responsibility for different decisions.

Training – ask your employer for training on management of stress and burnout. This is beneficial for both employee and employer. If your employer puts preventative strategies in place to manage and maintain stress levels this will in turn reduce instances of burnout which take longer to recover from.

Prioritising tasks and preparation – learn good time management skills and plan your work. Knowing what to expect from stressful situations will allow you to cope with things much more easily. Don't make knee-jerk reactions. See Chapter 6.

Take control – be confident in your role as a social worker and your ability to carry out your job. When you are vulnerable and unsure, stress makes you feel as though you are losing control. Being in control of your behaviour and your emotions helps you become more resilient and deal with adversity. Be positive and those around you will pick up on this – it's contagious!

Good communication – ensure that you know how to communicate with people. This will help you deal with conflict. Resolving conflict in a positive, healthy and constructive way can help diffuse stress and tension in the workplace or with service users. Be an active listener and pick up on body language and non-verbal cues; this improves relationships in all areas.

Healthy lifestyle – take responsibility for your physical and emotional well-being. Exercise regularly – this will improve your mental and physical health, lifting your mood and vitalising your mind and body, and it's also a great way to help you relax. Having a good sleep pattern, eating a healthy diet and cutting down on alcohol and cigarette intake are all good places to start.

Stay realistic – don't set unachievable goals – don't add unnecessary stress upon yourself by being a perfectionist and striving for things that are unrealistic. Just do your best.

Humour – social work is a very difficult job, often dealing with trauma, poverty, different aspects of abuse or even death; however, when it is appropriate it is OK to have humour in your work to help diffuse stress and lighten the mood.

Saying 'no' – sometimes it is important to say 'no' when people are putting additional demands on you. You may find it difficult to say 'no' to your boss but if you have reasons for this and can justify why you are saying no, most managers will take this into account. Explain that your workload is already stretched and if they want you to take on this new piece of work then they must help you prioritise the work you already have and look at which piece of work is most important. This can then be recorded in your case notes as to why something else took precedence.

Get a hobby – get yourself a hobby that you enjoy and that allows you to switch off and have time for you doing something that you really enjoy. Spend your 'free time' purposefully, allow yourself to have treats – tell yourself 'you deserve it', take time to get rid of bad habits. Spend time with loved ones.

Talking therapies – cognitive behaviour therapy may be necessary in more severe cases of stress and burnout, teaching you different techniques of relaxation and ways to change your behaviour.

ACTIVITY · WHAT ARE YOU GOING TO DO ABOUT IT?

Using the following headings, list how you are going to manage stress/burnout in these areas of your life:

Emotional   Physical   Practical

BURNOUT/STRESS MANAGEMENT TECHNIQUES

Instant fixes	Long-term strategies
Breathe deeply	Look after your body, mind and spirit
Take a walk outside	Meditation
Do something different	Regular exercise regime
Make a cuppa (for all!)	Good diet
Use positive affirmations	Have a regular routine
Visualisation	Adequate sleep
Desk exercises	Listen to music, sing!
Healthy snack	Plan your days
Have a laugh	Be organised
Take your lunch breaks!	Use support networks
Talk to your colleague	Have fun (lots)
Try not to dwell on things	Take your annual leave
Accept help when offered	Regular reality checks
	Learn to say 'no'

Your new habits

You should now have learned how to recognise signs and symptoms of stress and burn-out and developed strategies to overcome this. Make a note of the new habits you are going to take forward to help keep you healthy and safe.

Your Toolkit – Have a look at the Toolkit and think about your stressors, how you can recognise them, what you need to change or do differently and what you are going to do about it. Think about how you may address any issues with your line manager and how you use supervision here. Consider your support network and how you support others; note any evidence for your assessment.

TAKING IT FURTHER

Collins, S (2007) Social Workers, Resilience, Positive Emotions and Optimism. Practice, 19(4): 255–69 (www.tandfonline.com/doi/full/10.1080/09503150701728186?src=recsys)

Greer, J (2016) Resilience and Personal Effectiveness for Social Workers. London: Sage Publishers

Lomax, R, Jones, K, Leigh, S, Gay, C (2010) Managing Stress on Placement. In Surviving Your Social Work Placement. Basingstoke: Palgrave Macmillan, pp 95–108

Martin, GG (2012) Stress Management for Social Workers (Kindle Edition)

Stranks, J (2005) Stress at Work: Management and Prevention. Oxford: Elsevier Butterworth-Heinemann

8 Balancing your work and home life

INTRODUCTION

This chapter concentrates on encouraging you to enjoy your working life but to keep it as that – *your working life* – and nothing more. It is important that we enjoy our work but too much can definitely be a bad thing. When work crosses over into our personal life this can lead to a number of problems. Becoming qualified and getting a new job is exciting and scary at the same time and as a newly qualified worker you will be keen and want to make the best impression you can; this is normal. The danger is that you can get carried away and this can often mean that you take on too much – this can lead to the formation of poor habits and you becoming trapped in a cycle that can be difficult to escape from. All of us have been there at some point and found it difficult to manage and there will be periods in your career when things are more difficult than others. However, we all need to learn to recognise where the line is between our work and our home life and ensure that this boundary can be maintained. This may not always be possible but with a little thought and planning, we can achieve this for ourselves, for most of the time.

- o   What is work–life balance?
- o   Pressing the pause button
- o   Self-awareness
- o   Taking work home
- o   Setting boundaries
- o   Things to consider when looking at your own work–life balance
- o   Top tips

Links to:

PCF 1 – Professionalism

PCF 2 – Values and Ethics

PCF 8 – Contexts and Organisations

WHAT IS WORK–LIFE BALANCE?

It was not until the latter half of the twentieth century that there was any real recognition that a significant number of people within the working population had responsibilities outside of their work roles, and that such responsibilities could significantly impact upon their efficiency and productivity, and that, conversely, the demands of work could adversely affect employees' home life and reduce the quality and quantity of time workers could spend with their own families. One of the first pieces of legislation to address this directly came in the form of the Employment Relations Act (1999). Following this Act, the government commissioned three surveys looking at issues around and attitudes towards work–life balance – the baseline survey in 2000 (Hogarth et al., 2001) and two follow-up surveys in 2004 and 2007 (updated in 2011) (Stevens et al., 2004; Hooker et al., 2011). The surveys covered a number of years and demonstrated a clear increase in employees' interest in and expectations in terms of a better work–life balance and an increase in employers' policies to address this. There are a number of directives and laws that protect workers' rights in this area and perhaps the most significant one is the Working Time Directive 2003/88/EC, which sets out clear direction in areas such as holidays, break times and working hours (though it is possible for some workers to 'opt out' of this should they choose to). Originally, legislation and directives addressed the needs of particular groups of people such as carers and pregnant women, but more recently there has been a growing appreciation that all of us, no matter what our circumstances, need to be able to develop a work–life balance that addresses our individual needs and that we need to be supported in this by the organisation for which we work. For those of us working in stressful and demanding roles this is all the more important. For us to have a rewarding and fulfilling career this needs to be balanced with a happy and enjoyable home life.

A quick search on the internet reveals that most local authorities in their adverts for social workers promise a package of measures for new recruits to ensure a healthy 'work–life balance'. But what does this mean and how do they manage it? Usually the term is not that well defined but where it is, the measures can include flexible working, regular supervision, career progression routes, good training opportunities and more. There are clear benefits for employers who develop policies around positive work–life balance including improved staff retention, morale, well-being, attendance and loyalty. This can transfer into a better return in terms of training for staff and an increase in effectiveness and efficiency within the organisation. A happy and contented workforce is a productive and settled workforce.

There is no doubt that your employer has a responsibility in respect of work–life balance issues and it will be up to you to ensure that you take full advantage of what is on offer. However, you can do much to help yourself in this area and this chapter may help you in terms of thinking about achieving a healthy work–life balance (we will refer to it as WLB in this chapter). This is essential to your emotional and physical well-being as you progress through your career and will be key to your success as an effective practitioner. As a social worker you will work in a demanding and stressful workplace and it is crucial that you ensure that not only are you are fit to practise and provide a good service to your service users, but also that outside of the workplace you can enjoy quality time doing the things that you enjoy and have the freedom to deal with your responsibilities. We all owe it to ourselves and to others (both in and out of the workplace) to get this right. Social work is about supporting others and in order to do this you have a responsibility to support your own healthy lifestyle.

All of us have different elements to our lives and we have responsibilities and demands placed upon us from many areas. You may well have partners and children; some of you will provide care for older, sick or disabled family or friends, or have busy family lives, difficult and often stressful jobs, and perhaps your own health or disability issues to manage too. Additionally, you will often want (and need) to add a good mixture of a social life, hobbies and study or continuing professional development (CPD), not to mention the everyday, more mundane tasks that are required of us. No pressure then! The result can often be that your life becomes out of kilter and all too many times this begins with the demands of work encroaching physically or mentally into the other areas of your life.

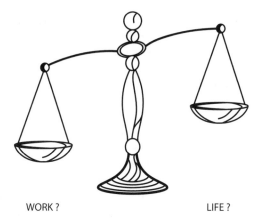

WORK ?   LIFE ?

A good way of thinking about WLB is to think of a set of scales – this gives you a clear picture of what your life is like when it becomes out of balance. Is your work weighing you down?

Sometimes it is obvious that things are not going as they should and this can be experienced as stress (see also Chapter 7) and its associated symptoms, in ourselves but also in others who may notice and tell you (either kindly or not so kindly) that things are going awry. Working late, going in early, thinking about work, bringing work home, not taking lunch or annual leave are all signs that things may not be quite right. You may find yourself having to deal with some comments from your colleagues when you take your lunch hour, because they have developed bad habits, including working through their lunch break. This is *your* time and you are given this for a reason. You need to take action before things get to this point and on a regular basis; this is another example of a good habit that we all need to develop. Beginning this at the start of your career will enable you to manage your WLB well and to achieve what you want to in both working and family life terms.

ACHIEVEMENT
(the things that we can accomplish)

ENJOYMENT
(an emotional state related to happiness)

WORK–LIFE BALANCE

Another way of thinking about WLB is in terms of 'enjoyment' and 'achievement' (www.worklifebalance.com/worklifebalancedefined.html). Those of you that work with young people will recognise this as one of the 'five outcomes' from Every Child Matters (a 2003 government initiative to ensure all children are given the support they need in order to thrive). We strive to ensure that young people (and we should apply this to all service users) 'enjoy and achieve' and we need to think of this in terms of ourselves too. Thinking in terms of what we want or need to achieve in any given time period alongside the need to do enjoyable things in life can be a helpful way of managing your WLB.

Think about this. It is a very simple concept and should be relatively easy to achieve. Once we are aware of the need for a positive WLB, and understand how to get there, we can develop our own simple strategies which will allow us to attain this balance. This will not be the same for everyone and for each of you this will change over time, depending on your own circumstances, needs and expectations. What follows are some simple ideas which you might find helpful in your own journey as you begin your social work career.

PRESSING THE PAUSE BUTTON

Having an awareness of how well your life is ticking along is crucial to the success that we all strive for. But once in a while you will need to stop and 'press the pause button'. In effect this means allowing some time to take stock of where you are at and how things are going for you. Using your skills in critical reflection will help you here. If things are going well, that's great, but it is always worth looking at what is going well and what it is that you are doing that is enabling this to continue. If things are not going so well, think about what has happened to make this the case and how you can change things to improve your lot. Check out the chapter on sources of support (Chapter 9) for ideas which may help you with this.

ACTIVITY • PRESSING YOUR PAUSE BUTTON

Make a list of the areas of your life that need to be balanced and where your responsibilities lie.

Draw a circle and imagine it is a cake. Divide your cake into sections in relation to how you would like your WLB to look.

Keep this and display it somewhere prominent – on the fridge, or in the front of your diary are good places.

Use this when you want to press your pause button.

If you are at a point where things are not going so well, draw another and compare the two.

We know that WLB will be different for all of you and that it is not static. Each of us is an individual and you will all want, expect and be able to cope with different things at different times in your lives. As an NQSW you will not be able to manage or be expected to manage a highly complex caseload – just for a second imagine adding into this your own home responsibilities, perhaps financial problems as a result of your student loan and sudden illness of a parent or child, and you can see how this could result in people not managing. There may be times when your own WLB is seriously out of kilter. The important thing is to recognise this and to 'press the pause button' and take stock. If you get into good habits and generally have a healthy WLB then when difficult times arise, you will be in a much better position to deal with them. Take control, be proactive rather than reactive and you will manage much better both in the short and longer term.

GOOD SELF-AWARENESS

It is important that you are able to read the signs that tell you that your WLB is out of sync. This might include you making mistakes, feeling stressed and tired, snapping at others, being late for appointments, a feeling of always being in a rush and never having enough time to complete tasks. Think about this in terms of job satisfaction – is this really what you want for yourself? What does this do for your motivation? There is plenty that you can do to address this situation – by looking after yourself, managing your time and developing positive habits, you will succeed. Look around the office and you will see others who work in this way but equally you will see others who are managing well, or even making the job look effortless.

It is important that you learn to give yourself feedback; think of yourself as a service user and make an assessment of what is happening in your life and why. Ask yourself how the day/week was, have a regular time for reflection – maybe your last hour on a Friday evening. Get into the habit of running through the week as a whole and thinking about how it feels. Use a 1 to 10 scale to quickly work out how you feel about things. Think about how you feel both physically and emotionally – are you a happy and contented tired person who is looking forward to the weekend or a stressed person wondering how you will enjoy the weekend with work still in your head (and possibly in your workbag at the side of you, too)? Another way to assess how things are for you is to catch yourself on a Monday morning and see how you are feeling about going into work. Reflect on your weekend and check that you have enjoyed it and achieved what you wanted to.

TAKING WORK HOME

The social work role is one that can be highly charged and extremely distressing at times, and we deal with some risky situations and people. You will no doubt be doing the job because you care about your service users a great deal. You are involved in their lives, sometimes on a daily basis, and also in making (often) life-changing decisions about them or with them. It is a great responsibility and one that can cause sleepless nights and will do for all of you occasionally. Emotionally, it is easy to get involved with service users and, though your training will have prepared you well for this, the reality is that there will always be some cases that you think about away from the office and this is quite usual. Where it becomes a problem is when your work keeps you awake constantly, and occupies large parts of your thinking and this starts to impact on your abilities both in and out of work. This is the time when you need to use your supervision well and to speak to your colleagues about your concerns. Generally speaking you should be able to go home at the end of the week and enjoy your time without work creeping into your thoughts.

Another one of the ways that people use to cope when things get too much for them at work is to begin to physically take work home with them – this is a sure-fire way of endangering your WLB, if you let it. If you find yourself in this position, press the pause button initially and take stock. Think about whether this is a good idea; remember that you are physically taking your work into your home environment. Is this what you want? Ask yourself, why am I doing this, is this a one-off, can I see this becoming part of a pattern, what impact will this have on my home life, what are the issues around health and safety and confidentiality here? There are many schools of thought on this topic and you will hear heated debates about this in the office. Have a look at the links below and see what you think. Watch and listen to your colleagues and you will see which side of the argument people are on. Our own training includes a debate on this issue and this always raises some interesting arguments both for and against taking work home. There are some offices where this is still somewhat acceptable and part of the culture of the team and some where it is very much frowned upon, and everything in between. Look at the chapter on managing your workload (Chapter 6) and see if this is helpful in working out any issues here.

One other thing – if you do decide to take work home with you, you will need to bear in mind the security of files and your laptop. Who in your home may have access to your equipment or files? Also consider any confidential telephone calls you may make to service users. Data protection is of huge concern for local authorities and if files and/ or laptops or memory sticks go missing the implications for both you and your employer could be severe.

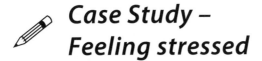

Case Study – *Feeling stressed*

As a social worker, Chris had always maintained that he would not take work home with him as he felt this was a sign that he had failed to manage his work within the allocated work time. He also felt that this was a line that he would not cross, that 'work was work' and that his own time was precious and was worth more to him. This worked well most of the time and he vowed that if he ever felt that he was in the position that he could not manage then he would seek another job.

Working as an agency social worker in a Children's Safeguarding team, Chris was given a number of cases which were in care proceedings and which required a lot of work, along with his other cases. As this was a new area to Chris he struggled to manage all of his work within his 37 hours. He became aware that he was making mistakes, forgetting things, and his job satisfaction and therefore motivation was low. Though he allowed time for things to settle, even after ten months this was still the case and he knew that this was not necessarily about him but more about the volume and pace of the work that was expected of him. Usually Chris was well organised, managed work very well and had always had positive feedback from managers about this in the past.

Chris eventually had no choice and felt that to enable him to continue he had to break his own golden rule and take a limited amount of work home, just for a while. He knew that he had crossed a line and resolved that he would do this in the short term, but planned and then did, actually seek an alternative post where the work was more manageable.

What do you think about the way Chris resolved this issue? Clearly this is one way that workers might deal with it and there will be others – what would you do?

NEW TECHNOLOGY

Being issued with a work phone and laptop is great, isn't it? Or is it? New technology can be at the same time a blessing and a curse. You will have the flexibility of working smarter and perhaps have to 'hot desk' or use touchdown points and you will be able to contact people without returning to the office to get access to a phone or the internet. The flip side of this is you are generally always available. How much and whether you let this affect your WLB will be for you to decide but there are some things to consider here – when do you turn off your work phone, do you do this in the car before you get into the house? Where do you leave your laptop, do you bring it into the house (as you are probably not allowed to leave it in the car anyway) but resolve not to get it out of its case? It's hard to resist the temptation to check in on your voicemail or emails when you are at home, especially if you are not going straight to the office. It then becomes difficult not to respond straight away – it's quiet in the car or at home and this can be better for calling people. There is a psychological angle at play here and an easy trap to get lured into. Once you have the computer open should you 'just write a few case notes?' If you have to do this, and the chances are you will at some point, then be aware of the pitfalls as well as any benefits.

USING YOUR TOIL WISELY

Some employers and especially those in the public sector operate a TOIL system. TOIL or 'time off in lieu' means exactly that – if you do additional hours you get to take them back; often there is a time limit on this so be careful. (This is one of the things that it is important to clarify during the job application process.) Get into the habit of keeping your records up to date daily (yes, it really is a pain!) and remember to put down your additional hours. They all add up – the odd 15 or 20 minutes may not seem much but over a week this could add up to an hour of time you are owed and your time is valuable to you and your family. Get into this habit and you will benefit from seeing just how your working week is spent and this is a great visual reminder when you are doing too much. Remember to take your TOIL record to each supervision session and plan with your manager how you are going to take this time back and when. It is tempting to let hours add up but beware of finding yourself in a position where you are not able to take this time for service reasons as you could very well lose out. If you do choose to start work at 8am instead of 9am your manager may say that this is not time you can accrue in TOIL, and that it is your choice to start early – this may be the case in some teams.

SETTING BOUNDARIES

Setting boundaries around your work is a healthy way for 'work to stay work' and not encroach on your home life. Think about the issues that have been raised in this chapter and consider how you can ensure that your WLB is protected. Start as you mean to go on. It may be that you want to be flexible and perhaps don't mind the odd bit of report writing at home or it may be that your golden rule is never to bring work home whatever the reason or situation. We are all different and our own personal boundaries will be different at different times too. The most important thing is our awareness to the possibilities of what can become a real issue and an early warning system to tell us when things are not going well.

THINGS TO CONSIDER WHEN LOOKING AT YOUR OWN WLB

- How do you switch off? What personal time do you enjoy?
- Have you got a hobby which takes you away from the social work world?
- Do you have friends that are unconnected to work?
- Do you discuss your work at home – however confidentially?
- Do you take regular leave or let the leave year go by without noticing?
- Do you accrue too much TOIL or make the most of your flexitime?
- Is your partner in the same type of work? – beware the two of you don't get sucked into talking about work-related issues.
- Do you have a healthy diet, a regular and sensible sleep pattern, and take regular exercise?
- Do you laugh a lot? Are you happy and positive?
- Do you surround yourself with positive influences?
- Is your home a safe and calming place to be where you can relax and enjoy being you?
- Is there anything else that you can think of?

The purpose of this list is to enable you to think and to take stock of your own situation. Be proactive and you will be successful in achieving a good WLB – most of the time!

You will see that some of the above are also discussed in the chapter on stress and burn-out – which will often be the result if you do not get the WLB on track.

ACTIVITY • DO YOU WORK TO LIVE, OR LIVE TO WORK?

Look at the question above.

Now look at it again.

Think about what it really means to you.

Is work something that you do to support living life the way you want to?

Or ...

is it the sole focus of your whole life?

The best news is – it's easy to balance the scales once you know how.

OUR TOP TIPS FOR ENSURING A HEALTHY WORK–LIFE BALANCE

- Press the pause button regularly.
- Know your limits and your patterns.
- Listen to your body and listen to others.
- Really think about whether you ought to take work home with you.

Your new habits

Now that you are aware of the need to balance your work and home life, we encourage you to think about how you will take this forward. Think about what you can do in the short and longer term to ensure that your life stays in balance in the future and how you will recognise if this is not the case and build this into your practice.

Your Toolkit – How does your work life impact on your home and vice versa? What evidence do you have that you are proactive in ensuring a healthy WLB and how does this positively affect your service users and yourself?

TAKING IT FURTHER

Websites:

www.communitycare.co.uk/2014/06/15

www.metro.co.uk/news/902469-screen-slaves-who-take-work-home-risk-mental-and-physical-health

www.worklifebalance.com/worklifebalancedefined.html

Your sources of support

INTRODUCTION

This chapter explores the support systems that are in place to help you become and remain a professional social worker. Areas covered include different types of support – family members, friendships, peer support, and support from practice educators and supervisors – and we guide you to external sources of information and support from professional agencies. We will look in detail at how to get the most from supervision, give you an insight into the complexities of supervision for you and your organisation, and include a brief discussion on clinical supervision. We will look at the importance of 'reflective practice'. We also include some theory during the chapter to consolidate your learning.

- o Different types of support
- o Professional agencies and websites
- o Why have supervision?
- o Supervision and your ASYE
- o Situational leadership
- o Types of supervision
- o Clinical supervision
- o The functions of supervision
- o Influences on your supervision
- o Reflective practice

Links to:

PCF 1 – Professionalism

PCF 5 – Knowledge

PCF 7 – Intervention and Skills

PCF 6 – Critical Reflection and Analysis

PCF 9 – Professional Leadership

DIFFERENT TYPES OF SUPPORT

Throughout this book we have talked at length about how important it is to have support networks and strategies in place to support you in your role as a social worker (see Chapters 7 and 8).

There are many different types of support but you must find those that suit you best.

- It is important to have friendships out of social work if possible so that you are able to switch off from your work and not talk 'shop' all of the time. People who are not involved in social work do not want to hear about your work; this would not be professional and would break all the rules around confidentiality. Switch off when you leave the office.

- Your partner can be a good source of support. However, if they also work in social work, don't get bogged down by talking about work issues. If your partner does not work in social work they may not understand the type of pressure you have been involved with during your day, therefore may not be as supportive to you as perhaps you would like. However, this may mean that it allows you to switch off from work and not take work into your home environment. You could agree that if you come home and you need time out for half an hour to 'wind down' that they know and understand why this is the case, and then you can give them your full attention later. We recognise you may not have the luxury of having a spare half hour when you get home if you have to get the tea and family sorted out.

- Family and friends offer different types of help and support and having different friends to do different activities with or just to meet and have a cuppa with is great. You can focus on them and have fun too, which will help you if you are having a particularly difficult time at work.

- Use your colleagues as support. You can ask them for advice about the cases you are working on and you will soon find out who in the team you feel comfortable approaching. Have a look around your team and see how this mutual support is offered without people actually realising. As colleagues you will talk about your cases and what is working well and not so well and often your colleagues may also have held those cases in the past, particularly those families that have been in the system for many years. Your colleagues will understand your difficulties. At the same time, however, be careful not to turn into the office whinge and just complain about everything and everyone. Be sensible and no doubt they'll support you.

- As an NQSW you could form a group with other NQSWs in your organisation to give one another mutual support. However, your organisation should be putting arrangements in place such as social work forums to give additional support to NQSWs. Students should be able to access support through your local students' union as well as directly through your university.

- Practice educators are very experienced social workers who are knowledgeable and are trained to be able to offer supervision and teaching and undertake assessments of social work students. They will have a great understanding and awareness of life as an NQSW, particularly about some of the feelings and emotions you are experiencing.

- Your team manager is a major source of support, which we consider within the supervision aspect of this chapter.

- Many organisations have other support groups such as Gay and Lesbian Groups or Black Workers Groups. If you fit this category and want to find out more, go along to one of their meetings, you'll be very welcome.

- The Human Resources (HR) department will help support you on certain issues. HR is the division of the organisation that focuses on the employees. They get involved with recruitment and retention of staff, disciplinary procedures, orientation and training and will advise on certain policies around your employment rights and benefits. Payroll is also a department that will offer advice. You may have a pension scheme that will be linked to your job, and advice and support will be available around these aspects of your future employment, either by the pension administrator directly or initially via HR or payroll.

- The Occupational Health department deals with promoting and maintaining your optimal physical and mental health and your social well-being alongside your health and safety at work. This includes checking that adaptations are in place to allow you to undertake your job and making sure that risk assessments are carried out to ensure you are safe and prevent health departures due to working conditions.

PROFESSIONAL AGENCIES AND WEBSITES

There are many professional agencies and commercial organisations that offer different types of support including advice around working conditions and your rights as a worker, and those that give specific support for social workers. Here is a list of some of those agencies:

- *Community Care Inform* – This is an online resource for social workers to access regarding a variety of things such as new legislation and research and allows you to make decisions based on evidence.
www.ccinform.co.uk

- *Community Care* is a useful website. It has articles and up-to-date news on all sectors of social work and research, including jobs.
www.communitycare.co.uk

- *The British Association of Social Workers* has a great website offering training and support and membership includes training, insurance and a new social workers union representation. There are fees for a full service but you can get general advice from the website.
www.basw.co.uk

- *Social Care Institute for Excellence (SCIE)* – This is a charity that translates the knowledge and experience of service users into practical resources for social care staff to use to improve practice. Social Care TV developed by SCIE can be useful for learning and training with lots of great online videos you can watch across all disciplines of social care. All SCIE resources are free to download; however, to access some downloads you will need a free MySCIE account. See   www.scie.org.uk/socialcaretv/ and www.scie.org.uk.

- *The Department for Education* is responsible for education and children's services. It has an academies programme which provides schools with greater freedom to innovate and raise standards. The website provides the current legal position regarding educational issues, historical information, research and case studies that schools or workforces have found useful.
www.education.gov.uk

- *Directgov* offers disabled people information on a wide range of topics on disability rights. In the 'disabled people' section, you can find out about:

  - the Disability Discrimination Act;

  - the Disability Rights Commission;

  - Equality and Human Rights Commission and the Office for Disability Issues (ODI);

  - international disability rights.
    www.disability.gov.uk

- *Unison* is the UK's largest public service union, representing more than 1.3 million people, and provides vital services to the public. It offers various levels of membership and gives access to a whole range of benefits, from free legal and welfare advice to discounts on insurance and grants for workplace training.
www.unison.org.uk

- *The Law Society* provides information to help find the right legal support you need. They offer a range of products and services to help you in practice.
www.lawsociety.org.uk

WHY HAVE SUPERVISION?

Supervision is a key element of how you function as a social worker and how effective you can be in making positive changes to the lives of your service users, regardless of which area of social work you practise in. Supervision links into all of the PCF domains, allowing you to use supervision as a holistic tool for planning, safeguarding and facilitating change. Supervision should also be a link with the HCPC's Standards of Proficiency.

The now defunct Social Work Reform Board in 2012 identified that supervision should:

- improve the quality of decision making and interventions;
- enable effective line management and organisational accountability;
- identify and address issues related to caseloads and workload management;
- help to identify and achieve personal learning, career and development opportunities (http://webarchive.nationalarchives.gov.uk/20140109082940/http://education.gov.uk/a0074263/swrb/a0074263/standards-for-employers-and-supervision-framework).

Definition of supervision:

> **Supervision is an accountable process which supports, assures and develops the knowledge, skills and values of an individual, group or team. The purpose is to improve the quality of their work to achieve objectives and outcomes. In social care and children's services this should optimise the capacity of people who use the service to lead independent and fulfilling lives.** (Skills for Care and Children's Workforce Development Council (CWDC), 2007, p 5)

The now defunct Social Work Reform Board in Munro (2011b, p 53) state:

> **Supervision is an integral element of social work practice not an add-on. Through it social workers review their day-to-day practice and decision making, plan their learning and development as professionals, and work through the considerable emotional and personal demands the job often places on them.**

Recommendation 11 in Munro (2011c) states: *training and supervision of Social Workers should be clear about the capabilities needed for social work.*

SUPERVISION AND YOUR ASYE

In your new role it is important that supervision is pitched at the appropriate level for your understanding and development. Don't try to 'run before you can walk'. You should enjoy this time because if you rush and try to take on work that is too complex your confidence will be knocked and mistakes could be made, which could have serious implications for your career as a practising social worker and for your service users. Your supervisor should recognise your maturity in your social work role and gear supervision and support to the appropriate level, developing your competence and confidence. Supervisors and managers should effectively facilitate and promote opportunities for your development and learning on a day-to-day basis.

Having already discussed Emotional Intelligence in Chapter 5, we reflect here on why it is important to ensure you are using your 'emotional intelligence' (EI) within your supervision. Your manager should help you to understand the link between EI and supervision. Whichever area of social work you are working in, you are no doubt working with those most vulnerable in society and the decisions and judgements you make on your cases impact on your service users. Many of these decisions are huge. Let's think about those for a moment – you may be having to remove a child from their family home or making a decision about a person's mental capacity. You must ensure that you are emotionally intelligent in your supervision session because this is when you are talking and reflecting about each of your cases and making some of the most important decisions about other people's lives – therefore you need to be 'emotionally' in tune with yourself, your service users, your managers and your organisation. It is crucial to talk with your supervisor about any concerns, worries and anxieties you may have about your cases. This includes dealing with hostile and difficult service users including those deemed aggressive and violent and where you may be frightened or those cases where you are simply feeling out of your depth managing significant risks and/or feeling out of control. If you do not talk about these difficulties in your supervision this will breed a culture of dishonesty, put you and others at risk and increase stress and anxieties. People who are in highly stressful situations and do not confront their feelings often continue to work but become detached, unemotional and often inhumane. This is dangerous for you, your colleagues and service users. You need to be able to self-reflect and understand yourself and what makes you 'tick' before you can effectively understand other people. If you are not, this will in turn impact on poor decision making and produce negative outcomes for all concerned (Morrison, 2005; Wonnacott, 2012).

It is important, too, to ensure you are acutely aware of any conflict between your personal and professional values and ethics and that you discuss this within your supervision as soon as they arise. (See Chapter 3.)

SITUATIONAL LEADERSHIP

Hersey and Blanchard (1988) developed a model of leadership called 'situational leadership' which is useful for you to know about in order to understand why your manager should be pacing you and gradually increasing the complexities of your workload at a level to suit you.

Situational leadership looks at four levels of maturity that as a social worker you will progress through. These levels are Telling, Selling, Participating and Delegating (Hersey and Blanchard, 1988):

- *Telling.* As an NQSW your supervisor will need to 'tell' you what is expected of you, give you reassurance and ensure that you are given the appropriate level of guidance. At this stage your supervisor is proactive and knows what work you are doing. They will seek to engage with you – keeping a tight rein.

- *Selling.* You will begin to understand more about the systems and the organisation you work within including constraints, resource implications and partner agencies. You will be linking theory to your practice and you will enter into more dialogue about the trajectory of your cases. Your supervisor remains heavily involved in directing you.

- *Participating.* Here you will be participating more in the decision making and coming up with solutions for your cases but your supervisor will still be aware of all the decisions that are being made and will maintain a high level of input in your relationship and your relationship with your service user.

- *Delegating.* In this stage, most of the decision making has now moved to you. Your supervisor will still have a good knowledge of what goes on in your cases but will sit more in the background and be more passive; however, you will not be abandoned.

Despite your levels of maturity increasing and safeguards being in place around your decision making, as a social worker YOU are still accountable for your part in the decision making process. You will be made 'accountable' should these decisions come under scrutiny in the future. You must always discuss any concerns you have with your supervisor. Be honest! This does not mean that they will think that you cannot do your job; they will appreciate this dialogue and either put in the additional support that you need to continue working on a case, or reallocate the case to a more senior member of the team.

ACTIVITY • WHY, HOW, WHAT – IN SUPERVISION

Before we look at supervision more closely, take ten minutes to think about and write down: why do you have supervision and what's its purpose? How often do you think you should have supervision? What types of things should you discuss in supervision (agenda items)? How does supervision link to case management and your progression? Also, think about any barriers to good supervision.
You can check your answers as we go through the rest of the chapter.

YOUR SUPERVISION CONTRACT

It is normal to have a 'Supervision Agreement' or 'Contract', which is usually a standard document agreed by yourself and your supervisor. This is where any specific agenda items can be outlined and agreed. Again, frequency of meetings would be identified within your contract. This contract or agreement is a working document that can be changed at intervals if necessary to ensure it is fit for purpose. The supervision contract should be in addition to your 'learning agreement' which you will sign up to with your employer and which describes how your employer will support you through your ASYE (see Chapter 11).

The Social Work Reform Board's 'Standards for Employers of Social Workers in England and Supervision Framework' suggests that an NQSW should receive weekly supervision for the first six weeks, fortnightly for the duration of the first six months and a minimum of monthly thereafter. As an NQSW you should have a protected caseload, particularly during your ASYE. You should have protected time for personal development, which normally equates to 10 per cent over the course of the year.

The Social Work Reform Board Standards state that supervision should last at least an hour and a half of uninterrupted time. It should be at an agreed time and venue. Your supervision should be held within a positive and safe environment, with trust and confidence being maintained by both you and your supervisor. Your supervisor will soon lose trust if you come out of the office and start telling your colleagues all about what you've discussed in your supervision. Your manager should give you feedback in a way that is constructive and that is open and honest but relayed in a positive manner so that you do not leave supervision feeling upset or humiliated. You should feel empowered and be able to discuss any concerns in relation to your work or issues that may impact upon your work or your health and well-being. Your planned supervision should be respected and not cancelled due to workload or other pressures of work. Don't get into the habit of thinking it's OK if your supervision is being cancelled due to other priorities. Your supervision is precious and important. If it is cancelled make sure you make another time as soon as possible and don't let it drift. If it is being cancelled regularly, you should talk with your manager about this.

TYPES OF SUPERVISION

Supervision can take place in more than one format.

- Group supervision – this may take place with you and several of your colleagues together. Supervision should be a tool for learning; for example, discussions around lessons learned from Serious Case Reviews, the Munro Report or recommendations from inspections.

- Ad hoc supervision – this is done on an 'as and when' basis. Most managers have an 'open door' policy so you can discuss issues with your manager as required, rather than waiting until your next supervision to check something out. Never be afraid to approach your manager.

- Individual supervision – this is your formal one-to-one time with your supervisor.

All key decisions made regardless of the type of supervision should be recorded on the service user's file, with a clear emphasis on who is taking what actions and any agreed timescales. You should also record any areas where you disagree. Your manager should be responsible for recording any 'management decisions' (Skills for Care and CWDC, 2007).

CLINICAL SUPERVISION

Clinical supervision is more often found within the wider health and social care settings such as adult mental health settings or nursing settings or the Child and Adolescent Mental Health Services (CAMHS). It is a formal process of professional support and learning which allows practitioners to develop competence and take responsibility for their own practice and to discuss complex cases in clinical situations. It encourages self-assessment and reflection and analytical skills. Clinical supervision is usually held in small groups of two or more practitioners, although the maximum number is usually six people, of the same or different professions. The professional leading the session does not have to be of a higher level but must have a sufficient level of skills, knowledge, experience and ability to develop others in the group. Specific cases and evidence-based approaches are discussed (Somerset Partnership NHS, 2016). If you are working in an environment that has clinical supervision, this should not replace your formal one-to-one supervision that we discuss in this chapter, and it should be given by someone who has a qualified social work background. Think about the differences between the two types of supervision and how you can learn from them both while working with a range of professionals within a multi-agency setting. They will also learn from you.

THE FUNCTIONS OF SUPERVISION

For the purposes of discussing supervision it is assumed here that your manager/supervisor is the same person. However, in some cases you may be supervised (ie, formal supervision and your day-to-day management responsibility) by a person other than the team manager.

You need to think about supervision as being a '*process*', and that you are part of this process. This includes the organisation, your manager and you as a student or newly qualified social worker and not forgetting the service users. Supervision has to meet the different agendas for each member within that process (Morrison, 2005).

There are four main interrelated aspects to supervision (Skills for Care and CWDC, 2007), which link to your ASYE learning agreement:

- line management (workload);
- professional supervision (reflective supervision);
- continuing professional development of workers (CPD);
- support (and protected time for personal development – 10 per cent).

Line management – this function of supervision should ensure that as an NQSW you are clear about your roles and responsibilities and importantly that the boundaries between you and your service users are clear. Your line manager will also look at the quality of your work and your output (how much work you actually do), and the outcomes. Your manager will ensure that you are working within the policies and procedures of the organisation/department. Your workload should be monitored to ensure that this is set at an appropriate level and your capabilities match the complexities of your caseload. Finally, your line manager should discuss any concerns around your practice. Deadlines and actions should be agreed.

Professional supervision – here you will look at management of your caseload. You should be given time to discuss and reflect on each of your cases with opportunity to clarify decisions. (We will discuss 'reflective practice' later.) Your line manager should ensure that you are demonstrating anti-discriminatory practice as well as discussing ethical and moral dilemmas and other issues such as diversity, religion and culture (these areas may interlink with line management issues too). Your supervisor should help you make decisions and ensure that you are safeguarding your service user, yourself and the organisation, focusing on managing risk, change and conflict. Together with your supervisor, you should ensure that clear risk assessments and individual service user care plans are in place. You should agree actions on your cases and check outcomes agreed in previous supervisions.

Continuing professional development – this will include identifying your learning and developmental needs or concerns. You should also discuss any issues raised within your annual appraisal (this may be known as something like PARD – Performance Appraisal Review and Development). These are the targets set for the following 12 months. It is likely you will not have one of these immediately. You may discuss your learning styles so that your supervisor is aware of how best you can learn and have new opportunities to learn. You should be given constructive feedback on your performance and how you interact and work as part of a team.

Support – this aspect of your supervision covers the more 'general' areas for discussion. This should include your annual leave, TOIL/flexi (which you must make sure that you take; see Chapter 8), sickness, health and safety, issues of equality and diversity including any issues around your culture or religion that your organisation should take into account, and any personal issues that may be impacting upon your ability to carry out your job. Supervision is not a counselling session but should be an integral part of a support network. This aspect of your supervision may be known as 'personal supervision' and recorded separately from case supervision.

You may want to do further reading on Models of Supervision and we would recommend you reading Morrison and Wonnacott (2010) (see 'Taking it further'). Here Morrison and Wonnacott discuss a more complex model of supervision and its functions. The 4 x 4 Integrated Model (or Framework) of supervision explores different elements of supervision to meet the needs of management, support, mediation and development.

We have devised a useful tool that you and your supervisor can use together to help identify and monitor risk: the NQSW's risks and resilience management tool; see Chapter 11.

INFLUENCES ON YOUR SUPERVISION

When you are in supervision you need to consider many of the wider implications that impact upon your supervision and decision making; this includes your past experiences both positive and negative. It is a good idea to think about your cases, and consider it as if the individual you are discussing is present, in person, in your supervision. Consider their needs and the situation they are in. Think not only about the 'here and now' but the 'future' and how you will reach the longer term goals and outcomes your service users want to achieve. You need to ensure you are clear about your role and the job you are doing and why. That may sound simple but it is very important. Also, consider the role of those you are working with and your colleagues in other agencies. Do you really know what they do and why? And, importantly, what is their role with the families you are involved with? Is this clear? Is everyone clear about what they are doing and why? You can then start to look at what is going on in your case and how you can move forward and resolve any issues. You also need to consider the frameworks and limitations that you

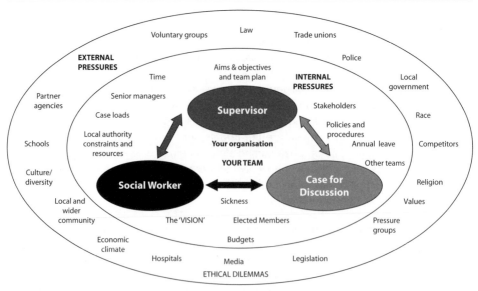

Figure 1 Who and what influences your supervision?

work within, such as legislation, policies and procedures and guidance. Also consider the broader factors that impact upon your supervision such as budgets, other agencies, the local community, etc (see Figure 1).

ACTIVITY • WHAT INFLUENCES YOUR SUPERVISION?

Take a few minutes to think about one of your more complex cases and the wider influences that impact upon your decision making that you must consider within your supervision. Consider all the different people and aspects of the case then check your answers with those identified in Figure 1. You may have come up with some that are not mentioned – that's OK, there's no right or wrong answers. Get into the habit of thinking about these influences when you are making decisions on your cases and within supervision. (Link this to the exercise on p 28 re Your Values and Ethics.)

REFLECTIVE PRACTICE

Reflective practice is an essential part of the support and learning that should take place within supervision. 'Critical Reflection and Analysis' is one of the nine domains of the PCF, with capacity statements built into all levels. We often have to challenge our existing opinions and thoughts; however, it is not always an easy process as new beliefs and opinions may compete with our current beliefs. This is something that you will do as you progress on your journey as a social worker and manage more complex cases. Sometimes we experience a 'discomfort' or 'discrepancy' between what we already know or believe and new information or interpretations, and we have to question our beliefs and accommodate new ideas to develop and open ourselves to new things. This is known as 'cognitive dissonance' (Festinger, 1957). Sometimes new learning can be blocked as we are committed to prior knowledge and feel safe with this, so we resist new learning. It is essential therefore that we all, regardless of what level we are practising, use reflective practice within supervision.

Seibert and Daudelin (1999) (pp 6–7), discuss the well-known theories of learning cycles established by Kolb in 1984 and Honey and Mumford in 1990. Seibert and Daudelin identify, and we concur, that learning results when *action and reflection are synthesized*, developing an intellectual understanding of a situation as opposed to a feeling, which is gaining knowledge about an experience and making sense of this experience and forming concepts and generalisations to guide future action. Active experimentation then takes place. In short, 'experiential learning' using 'reflective practice' takes place.

Therefore, in supervision you would discuss the following points.

1. You have an experience with your service user. This does not have to be a negative or unpleasant experience. You gain knowledge by having a direct experience.

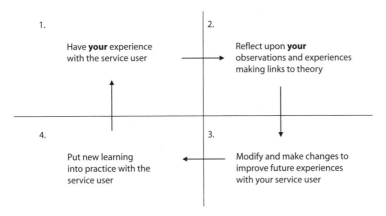

2. You have to reflect upon the experience, in supervision, and develop an intellectual understanding of your experience and the situation you were in. Think about your observations as part of that learning experience. Think how this fits with the theories you have learned within your social work training.

3. You make sense of the experience, understand it and form concepts to guide future actions. With your supervisor plan what to do when you have the same or similar experience again. Think of what you intend to do next time. Formulate new learning, concepts and planning.

4. Put your learning into practice when you visit your service user again. Your previous experience and reflection will now guide new experiences while working with your service user (Seibert and Daudelin, 1999).

Your learning continues following each experience and each case that you are working with simultaneously.

Daniel Kahneman (2012) talks about how it is important, when we are looking at a problem, that we use two distinct modes of reasoning that complement one another. In his book, *Thinking, Fast and Slow*, Kahneman talks about how we use two 'systems', those being: system 1, our *intuitive system* and system 2, our *analytical system*. While reflecting within your supervision your supervisor should ask questions to ensure you are not just using your 'system 1' and being intuitive and that you are being both intuitive and analytical together.

In system 1, our intuition works on its own and is never 'off', and although we are often right to trust our instincts, we can make errors and have bias. In order to aid our decision making we need to ensure that we take time to question our own thinking and use system 2 and analyse the situation. We do not have time to do this in all situations in everyday life, it would take too long. I'm sure your drive to work each day is mainly done on intuition and you don't have time to analyse everything, although we are sure at a roundabout you may do some quick analysis to see if the road is clear, but on the whole you are using your intuition. As a social worker, if you do not use both of these systems together, you are more likely to make errors. You are often working under tight deadlines and timescales, perhaps in a crisis, you might have a child protection investigation going on and you may not have all the information you need to inform your decision making and it is when the stakes are high that you are more likely to make mistakes. Therefore, it is essential to make sure, in supervision, that you have the time to *reflect* and use both system 1 and system 2 together and don't forget too, to draw on your emotional intelligence in the process (Kahneman, 2012).

The process of reflection upon your actions deepens during your development as your knowledge and understanding becomes greater.

Reflective practice should allow you to:

*   plan your cases;
*   look at different scenarios;
*   link theory and research to practice;
*   evaluate your decision making, why you made the decisions you did and the impact of your decision making;
*   revise hypotheses and plan what is to happen next;
*   consider the legal frameworks;
*   be intuitive AND analytical.

Case Study – Pushed to the limit

Alice worked in a busy older people's community social work team. She had worked in this team for about 12 years although only qualifying 15 months previously. Since qualifying Alice held a highly complex caseload including safeguarding cases. Alice never said 'no'. Alice was isolated working in a rural area, the sickness within the team was high and she seldom saw her colleagues and had only had supervision twice in seven months. Alice would work most weekends at home to catch up with cases and as she lived on her own she had become used to this lifestyle. Alice had some of her own health issues but ignored her own needs, instead focusing on her work. She began to struggle with the complexities of the cases and did not seek support, making risky decisions. Her supervisor had left her to it but then went on sick leave. It was a month before Alice was told that her manager was actually off on long-term sick leave. Alice was meeting deadlines due to the extra work she was doing at home but other work was continually being allocated to her via the electronic case management system until she held 50 cases. Alice went to work one morning and collapsed with exhaustion. She was off work for six weeks. Alice had been taken advantage of by the organisation, management and she'd allowed this to continue without asking for help. She had not been monitored in supervision. Her manager had expected that as Alice had so much previous experience she would automatically be able to take on complex cases now that she was a qualified social worker. This was totally unacceptable and a huge warning for everyone.

Think about this case – what could Alice have done to help herself and to prevent her collapse? Where and how could she have accessed support and at what points along the way?

Your new habits

There's a lot of information in this chapter that should help you along your journey and to get maximum support in your new job. Make a list of your new habits and think about planning your own support network. You may have a few ideas that you want to try straight away.

Your Toolkit – Look at the Toolkit and reflect on the things you have learned about supervision, and how you will get the most from your sessions. Consider how you will prepare for supervision and how your supervision benefits service users. How do you evidence your own professional decision making and your CPD within supervision?

 TAKING IT FURTHER

Field, P, Littler, L and Jasper, C (2016) Practice Education in Social Work. Achieving Professional Standards. Northwich: Critical Publishing (Chapter 5, pp 75–100)

Hawkins, P, Shohet, R (2012) Supervision in the Helping Profession, 4th edn. Maidenhead: McGraw-Hill

Morrison, T (2005) Staff Supervision in Social Care, 3rd edn. Hove: Pavilion Publishing and Media Ltd

Morrison, T, Wonnacott, J (2010) Supervision: Now or Never. Reclaiming Reflective Supervision in Social Work. Available online at www.local.gov.uk/c/document_library/get_file?uuid=545d7e64-f5b1-43a0-b4cb-46a03c7acce6&groupId=10180 (accessed 15 October 2016)

O'Rourke, R (2010) Recording in Social Work: Not Just an Administrative Task. Bristol: Policy Press

Wonnacott, J (2012) Mastering Social Work Supervision. London: Jessica Kingsley Publishers

10   Where will you go next?

INTRODUCTION

Once you have qualified, breathed a sigh of relief and finished celebrating, you may be thinking about what happens next. It may be that you have known all along what you want to do and you are working towards this. On the other hand, you may have thought you knew and now are not so sure, or you may have absolutely no idea! In any case this chapter is for you. Here we take a look at the options open for you now that you are a qualified social worker. You may know what is around, but we hope that this chapter will be of interest and give you new insight into the options for your new profession. We will also look at progression through the differing levels of social work from NQSW to manager level and beyond, and take a look at CPD and post-qualifying (PQ) options.

- The current climate
- Different levels and areas of social work
- Progression routes
- Continuing professional development
- Post-qualifying studies
- Working in the voluntary and statutory sectors
- Overseas working
- Agency working
- Independent working

ACTIVITY • WHAT DO I KNOW?

Get a piece of paper and list all of the things you know about working in social work and the different roles.

- How many areas of specialism can you list?
- What types or branches of social work have you come across?
- What job roles/names can you think of?

A WORD ABOUT THE CURRENT CLIMATE

As we write this, NQSWs are still facing challenging times in order to secure work in the statutory sector, which is where many NQSWs would like to work. We cannot ignore this and while we do not want to be negative, this is the reality for many at present. There are a multitude of reasons for this but for you this may make things more difficult (but certainly not impossible) to secure the job that you would like. There are a number of things that you might consider if you find yourself in this position.

- When you go for interview you need to be really on the ball and sell yourself well; there is a lot of competition and since you are the best candidate for the job you need to make sure that they know it – there are many books and resources around that will help you to do a great interview and presentation, if asked for.

- Try to think medium and longer term rather than short term. Remember that the job you get now can be thought of as a means to your long-term goal.

- Be flexible about your service user group and consider alternatives to your first choice.

- Think about widening your search in terms of the geographical area in which you would like to work.

- Consider temporary, part-time or job share, at least initially.

- Think about volunteering – this is also a great way to get experience and can often lead to paid employment.

- Although not ideal for you, give serious consideration to looking at unqualified positions – these will provide you with valuable experience and you are still using your social work knowledge and skills. It is often said that 'getting a job when you are in a job is always easier'.

One thing worth remembering is that the time spent looking for your work represents a gap in your CV and employers can often view this in a negative light.

An excellent resource for employment is www.compassjobsfair.com. Compass hold regular events throughout the country and have really good publications which will help you in your search. Attending one of their free events will count towards your CPD too.

It is also worth remembering that BASW run a mentoring scheme whereby NQSWs can be linked with an experienced social worker who will support them in their search for employment.

Remember that things are always changing in the job market and you will be able to get what you want – even if not straight away.

DIFFERENT AREAS OF WORK

There are many different areas of work that you can specialise in as a social worker but these generally fall into the following broad categories.

Children's work:
- Safeguarding children at risk
- Fostering and adoption
- Care management
- Parenting
- Youth offending
- Family court work (CAFCASS)
- Educational welfare
- Children with disabilities
- CAMHS (Child and Adolescent Mental Health Services)
- Young carers, advocacy and children's rights
- Working with children who are ill

Adult work:
- Care management
- Mental health including forensic social work
- Physical difficulties
- Learning difficulties
- Advocacy services
- Asylum seekers and refugees
- Homeless people
- Hospital social worker
- Drugs and alcohol

Apart from which service user group you want to work with, there are many other questions to consider during your job hunting such as:

- Do you want to be based in an office or in another building, perhaps a clinic or a hospital, or would you rather be out and about working in the community?
- Do you prefer short intensive work, perhaps completing assessments of some kind, or would you like to work in a long-term team where you need to develop ongoing relationships with service users that can last for years?
- Do you want to work full-time or would you consider part-time or job share?
- Do you want to work within a team working office hours or out of normal working hours or within a residential setting?

This is your starting point; consider the above and think about where you want to be in five years' time. Think about your five-year plan as a journey with your ideal job as the destination and plan how you are going to get there; you may want to plan in steps along the way in terms of your experience, which will be your steps to your perfect job.

LEVELS OF SOCIAL WORK

At this stage in your career you will be focused on getting your foot on the ladder but it is helpful to know about others' roles and how they fit together. The PCF is very helpful in setting this out in a clear way – which is something new for the profession. You can see that it is possible to work your way up in the world of social work to as far as you would like to go – even as far as the newly created post of Principal Social Worker, which every local authority now needs to have in place.

As you look at the PCF you can see that there are a number of levels of social work and you will see yourself currently at the beginning of your career, though not right at the bottom as you are now qualified. You can see that there are various titles for social workers at different levels and when you are searching for work you will come across others; for example, sometimes an experienced social worker can have the title 'senior social worker' or 'lead practitioner'. This can be very confusing as different workplaces often have different names for the same role. Generally speaking, as an NQSW you will be given the title of social worker.

PROGRESSION ROUTES

As you become more experienced you will hear people speak about 'progression'. They are talking about how you move up through the levels or grades of social work as you become more experienced and take on more responsibility, and what you need to do in order to progress to the next level. As you become more knowledgeable and your skill level develops, you will be expected to work with more complex cases and ones where the levels of risk are considerably higher and this is reflected in a higher grade and usually a higher pay scale. Your progression will depend on your ability to:

- manage different complexities of risk;
- safeguard service users and manage conflict;
- model good practice;
- enable others;
- use your own initiative and make autonomous decisions;
- be confident and have the ability to challenge;
- increase your knowledge of your organisation and strategic planning;
- manage a higher level of complex cases;
- support other workers within the team;
- manage change in difficult and complex situations;
- use reflective practice and make judgements;
- engage in critical and complex decision making;
- work in multi-agency and collaborative settings;
- link theories to practice and produce comprehensive assessments.

Routes to progression can vary within different organisations and if you are in statutory employment, it varies within different local authorities. Employers with whom we have consulted are still in the process of developing their career structures in line with the PCF structure and the new PQ framework. These developments are certainly significant changes for the social work profession and for your career progression and things continue to look very positive in this respect.

CONTINUING PROFESSIONAL DEVELOPMENT (CPD)

Historically (though now quite unbelievably), a social worker could qualify and then continue to practise without ever having to prove that they had undertaken any further training. Thank goodness those days are now behind us and there is an all-round recognition of the need to continue to learn and develop throughout our career (though many of us have always known this and continued our learning as we have gone along). As we know, CPD is a vital component of our work and essential now in order to keep registered and continue in practice as a professional.

The HCPC will want to see the evidence that you have continued to learn, and the responsibility not only to ensure that you do so but also that you are able to evidence this rests entirely with you as the practitioner. Your employer can encourage, support and enable you but you are the one who must ensure your continued development. The HCPC will also want to see that you have taken advantage of a range of different learning opportunities including:

- formal training courses and seminars;
- shadowing other colleagues from other teams or organisations;
- reading and research;
- reflecting on practice;
- supervision discussion;
- discussions with colleagues;
- learning by having new experiences;
- presenting to a team meeting.

There are many others and these can be found on the HCPC website.

It is important that you see CPD as a continuing process and are able to bring forward the learning needs identified in your last placement and in your practice portfolio while at university. These should be transferred into your ASYE agreement; at the end of your ASYE you should again carry these forward on an annual basis with your supervisor and these should be discussed and recorded in supervision and in your annual appraisal/ review.

In order to fulfil the requirements for CPD it is important to start as early as you can and ensure that this is a habit that you get into now. Keep good and clear records of your CPD in a separate file and keep it up to date; otherwise we can guarantee (from our own experience!) that you will miss something out and when you come to renew your registration you will be selling yourself short and may be scratching your head trying to remember stuff too!

POST-QUALIFYING STUDIES (PQ)

In terms of post-qualifying training there is a recognised pathway to complete more formal and qualifying studies once you have completed your ASYE.

The Post Qualifying Framework for Social Work Education and Training (2005) defines the general requirements for all current PQ programmes, though there is no standardised programme across the country with most organisations coming together with educational providers to deliver locally developed courses under the framework.

PQ models usually include the following, depending on your chosen pathway:

- children and young people, their families and carers;
- leadership and management;
- practice education;
- social work in mental health services (includes approved mental health professional);
- social work with adults.

Some modules can often be taken on a 'free standing' basis; other modules are core mandatory elements of the PQ, such as the 'Consolidation' module which, as it sounds, consolidates social workers' previous knowledge including their value base and skills learned to date, and helps them apply this to their post-qualifying practice.

For those who completed their social work studies at a BA level it is possible to increase this to a Masters degree, again following your chosen pathway, using PQ studies to achieve this. The local university will have details of this on their website.

Many social workers reach the stage in their career where they want to pass on their knowledge and skills to others and move into supporting students in a Practice Educating role. There is also an expectation within the PCF that as you progress to 'experienced' and 'advanced' level that you 'model', 'foster' and 'support' an environment that promotes learning and practice development within the workplace. The Practice Educator Professional Standards for Social Work (PEPS) provide the overarching guidance for the teaching, assessing and supervision of social work degree students. All practice educators of social work students must be registered social workers. A good source of information for anyone interested in this work is *Practice Education in Social Work* by Field, Jasper and Littler (2016).

As the government continues to introduce changes, in line with the development of the PCF and its post-qualifying frameworks, it is advisable that social workers wishing to undertake post-qualifying training discuss the different routes and modules with their own training and development department and their local universities. You may also be eligible for prior learning and education to be taken into account under Accredited Prior Learning (APL), Accreditation of Prior Experiential Learning (APEL) and/or Accreditation of Prior Certificated Learning (APCL) and Advanced Standing. There is lots of information available online by searching Skills for Care, BASW and HCPC as well as your local university websites.

WORKING IN THE VOLUNTARY AND STATUTORY SECTORS

There are many opportunities to work as a social worker in both the statutory sector and voluntary sector (sometimes called the third or charity sector) and you may have already come across this in your placements. Though the statutory sector is by far the largest employer of social workers, there are some roles in the voluntary sector; for example, many of the larger national charities have social work posts and these will be advertised as such. In other jobs in the voluntary sector, workers in these roles may not be called social workers but may be called project workers, development workers, community workers and many, many others. You can gain great experience working in the voluntary sector and this work gives you an insight into working with service users who often really want to work with you, unlike in the statutory sector where sometimes they are compelled to and can occasionally be resistant and hostile – this can lead to a very different work experience and is well worth considering.

The issues around funding posts can be difficult in the voluntary sector as often posts will be advertised as short term and can be dependent on funding continuing. In the current financial climate many voluntary sector organisations have had funding cuts and this has had an impact not only on service provision but also on recruitment of staff. Terms and conditions for workers in the voluntary sector can vary, with many having similar terms to local authority ones, but it is always worth checking this out.

Working in the statutory sector for a local authority or perhaps a Clinical Commissioning Group can bring more job stability and security and will often have good terms of employment and offer more permanent positions. Once you are employed by a local authority you can often move between teams and disciplines and if you decide to move to another local authority and sometimes larger voluntary organisations, you can usually take such things as your accrued holidays and pension rights across to your new employer. As a local authority employee you usually have access to high quality and frequent training courses.

OVERSEAS WORKING

You will often see adverts for social workers for overseas in magazines or on the internet. This can be a great opportunity to see the world and gain experience of other working cultures at the same time. Often relocation fees will be paid and interviews will be carried out in this country. It can be a long and complicated process but can have great rewards. Most countries who advertise have similar laws to our own and often, registered social workers within the UK, with UK qualifications to degree level, are able to work overseas, for example, in Australia, New Zealand, USA and Canada, without having to top up their qualification, but you should check with the employer and the social work governing body prior to considering these jobs. You may also need to complete a language and skills test as a part of the recruitment process.

- Australia
  The Australian Association of Social Workers (AASW)
  www.aasw.asn.au/

- New Zealand
  Aotearoa New Zealand Association of Social Workers (ANZASW)
  http://anzasw.org.nz
- USA
  National Association of Social Workers
  www.socialworkers.org
- Canada
  Canadian Association of Social Workers
  www.casw-acts.ca

There is a lot to consider before working overseas. Most countries that are looking for overseas social workers will want a high calibre social worker with experience. Therefore, if you are considering working overseas, you may want to consider this a little further along in your career. You will be competing with social workers from their country of residence in some countries who are still experiencing the recession, but don't be put off; if this is something you really want to do, go for it. But first and foremost you must have the correct visas for the type of work and the country where you wish to pursue your social work career. Have a look at the country's immigration website for further information about working and visas in the country of your choice; it will offer you a host of advice and tell you about the criteria you have to meet.

Some important things to consider here include:

- visa requirements, work permits;
- fees;
- your financial situation;
- accommodation;
- your age;
- skilled migration schemes;
- qualifications required;
- length of any proposed contract.

You may also want to consider:

- the different culture;
- weather/climate;
- working with different legislation;
- distance from UK/family and friends and time difference;
- the emotional impact of such a move;
- your support networks – both in and out of work;
- opportunity for having new experiences;
- cost of living.

AGENCY WORKING

Working through an agency on a temporary contract is one alternative to being employed on a permanent basis. This can be a great way to gain experience of a number of different roles, and if you are up for a challenge and enjoy change then this may be the ideal way forward for you. Sometimes, though, because you may be filling in for someone who may have gone off suddenly or there are additional pressures in the team which have required an agency worker to be placed, there can often be an expectation that as an agency worker you will 'just get on with the job' and you can occasionally be offered less support in these roles – which is not ideal as an NQSW. Additionally, you may find it more difficult to meet the requirements of your ASYE working though an agency, so check this out if you are considering this option.

There are two ways that you can be placed as a worker by an agency. Either you can work for the agency, in which case you are effectively employed by them and they deduct your tax and national insurance, or you can form a limited company, in which case you are responsible for your tax affairs and dealing with the tax office. This is a very simplified view and setting up a company is fairly easy but can have some serious implications if you don't get it right. There are special tax rules that apply to people who work as agency workers and we would urge anyone considering this route to seek advice before taking this step.

There is a common perception that temporary agency workers earn more money than their employed work colleagues. This may be true if you look only at the hourly rate you are paid, but you need to balance this with the things that you may *not* get as an agency worker. The Agency Workers Regulations (AWR), which were introduced in October 2011, brought about an improvement in agency workers' rights and these will affect you if you are in the same or similar role for over 12 weeks. If you are considering this as a way forward then we would encourage you to have a look at the guidance for AWR (see 'Taking it further', below). There are many agencies around that will place you on a short-term contract basis with a service user (eg within a team or role) and we would encourage you to talk with more than one of them as each will offer a slightly different service.

Remember too that recruitment agencies can also find permanent positions for social workers and working within a team for an agency can give you a head start in knowing what jobs will be advertised in the future; often this can lead to you securing a permanent role within the team. At present there are fewer opportunities for NQSWs to work on a temporary basis as there are many experienced workers who are looking for work due to the local authority cuts and reductions in some social work departments. Agencies may also help to get you into temporary unqualified roles in the meantime, though.

INDEPENDENT WORKING

A growing number of social workers are choosing to work totally independently. This means that you seek your own work in your own time and are your own boss, running your own business. You are responsible for your book-keeping and tax affairs and ensuring that you are professionally insured. Other things that you would need to consider if you chose this option would be access to professional supervision, completing your CPD and maintaining your registration, data protection and issues around your own health and safety. Working independently by its nature can be quite isolating so contact with others is vital in this role.

This way of working gives you great flexibility but you need to work hard to network and develop a good reputation for yourself. For this reason many independent social workers have worked for years before taking this step and have established good professional relationships which can help in securing work once they become independent.

Independent social workers generally work in one of two different ways, either directly with service users on a commissioned basis or as a consultant, expert witness in court, or in an investigatory or advisory capacity. There are a number of organisations set up by and for independent practitioners including Nagalro (Professional Association for Children's Guardians, Family Court Advisers and Independent Social Workers; www.nagalro.com). A search of the internet will bring many resources for your information if you want to look into this further.

There are some independent workers who are beginning to come together in groups and to bid for pieces of work or particular services in some areas. This kind of work is still in its infancy but is likely to develop over the next few years.

CONCLUSION

Now that you have read through this chapter, how are you feeling – are you surprised/ inspired/confused – a little bit of all three? As you can see, there are lots of options available to you now that you are a qualified and registered social worker. We have tried to give you a little more insight into what is on offer and the opportunities out there which can provide you with a wide-ranging and lengthy career. We hope that you are not now spoiled for choice; this is by no means a complete list of options, rather just a little something to whet your appetite.

TAKING IT FURTHER

Field, P, Jasper, C, Littler, L (2016) Practice Education in Social Work: Achieving Professional Standards. Northwich: Critical Publishing

Websites:

www.gov.uk/government/uploads/system/uploads/attachment_ data/file/32121/11-949-agency-workers-regulations-guidance.pdf

11 Supporting your NQSW through the ASYE

INTRODUCTION

This chapter is slightly different from the others in the book in that it has a different focus – which is not to say that it will not be useful for NQSWs to read. This chapter offers some support and guidance to those of you who have the job of assessing NQSWs during the ASYE and making a recommendation of a pass or fail at the end of that year – quite a responsibility.

o   Who is an assessor?
o   Where do I begin?
o   Having a structure
o   Dealing with difficulties
o   Useful exercises
o   Your own support network

The purpose of this chapter is not to repeat information that is freely available from a variety of other sources (your own local policy and procedure, the internet, professional books and journals, colleagues, for example) but to supplement this with some basic guidelines around good practice and to point you in the right direction in terms of where to start. We will also offer some exercises that you may wish to complete with your NQSW at various points in the assessment process.

The ideas in this chapter will probably not be new to most, nor are they complicated, but we hope they provide you with a framework or perhaps act as a refresher as we all begin this new journey together. We hope that this chapter will have something for everyone regardless of your experience and you will all have your own particular and specialist knowledge and skills which will assist in your work with our newly qualified colleagues.

Remember also that we are talking here about the 'assessment' of the NQSW though their ASYE, but the assessment is not just about supervision and a written report. It is about ensuring that you create an environment where the NQSW has the opportunity to develop throughout the year. This can only be achieved by providing an integrated package which also includes your commitment to:

- the learning agreement;
- encouraging reflection;
- allowing developmental time;
- regular supervision;
- workload management;
- a professional development plan;
- regular reviews of progress.

Your responsibility as the assessor is to ensure that all of this is in place, and ongoing for the NQSW.

WHO IS AN ASYE ASSESSOR?

The only formal requirement to be able to assess an NQSW on the ASYE is that you are a qualified and registered social worker. In this respect all of us will be more than familiar with the requirements of the assessment process as this is the basis of all of our work.

There may be times when the role of the assessor and manager/supervisor is split, perhaps when the NQSW's manager is not a qualified and registered social worker. This may pose particular challenges for all concerned and clear and regular communication and recording will be even more crucial in this case to enable the process to run smoothly.

Some of you will have been managers, supervisors or assessors in other roles; but there may be others of you who are totally new to the assessment of a worker rather than a service user. The principles of assessment are the same as you will have used before – a systematic way of gathering information during the year, which will then be analysed and which will inform your final recommendation.

BEFORE YOU BEGIN YOUR YEAR OF ASSESSMENT

It might be useful for you, before you begin, to 'press the pause button' and ask yourself the following questions:

1. How confident do I feel in this role?
2. What would make me feel 100 per cent confident?
3. What do I need to do to fill the gap between 1 and 2 above?

4. What resources do I need to fulfil my role?
5. Where will I find this information/gain this knowledge?
6. What support is there for me in this role?
7. Am I ready?

Only when you have addressed these questions and feel ready should you begin your work with the NQSW. We all like to jump ahead, especially with the pressure of work as it is, but it is really important that you allow yourself the time to address these questions and to feel comfortable before you begin in your role as assessor. You need to feel ready and prepared for your role.

SETTING OFF ON THE ASYE JOURNEY

Remember – we are all busy professionals but clearly this is an important step for NQSWs and we need to be aware that how we manage and supervise newly qualified workers now will set the tone for their future careers and should give them a professional start from which to build upon.

If your assessment is a part of the overall supervision of the NQSW, then you both need to be familiar with the Standards for Employers of Social Workers in England in relation to the requirements for supervision. This will ensure that your supervision is carried out professionally and will provide support and guidance for you as a supervisor and ensure the best experience for the NQSW; you will also need to be familiar with the Knowledge and Skills statements for your work setting as this will form an integral part of your assessment along with the PCF.

Before meeting with the NQSW for the first time – the practicalities

1. Address the questions above as a first step.
2. Talk things through with your own manager.
3. Set up a file on the computer and a paper file if required.
4. Read all documentation thoroughly, including the new Supervision Standards.
5. Ensure that team colleagues are aware of the ASYE, what this entails and how they can support new workers.

The first session

1. Start as early as you can after appointment with your NQSW.
2. Set regular times for meetings for the year, with review times built in from the beginning.
3. Find out if the NQSW is undertaking other induction training as a new employee and link into this so as not to duplicate work.

4. Go through the assessment/Knowledge and Skills statement/PCF etc together to ensure you both understand the documents and processes.
5. Be clear on the written agreement.
6. Be clear about what you can and cannot offer.
7. Be clear about what the NQSW can expect from you and what you expect from them.
8. Ask how they are feeling about the year ahead.
9. Complete a year plan which includes dates for the year ahead.

AS YOU GO ALONG

1. Stick to meeting times.
2. Encourage and give positive feedback, share your thoughts, be constructive.
3. Ask colleagues and service users for their feedback.
4. Keep up to date with recordings.
5. Seek out different and appropriately challenging opportunities for your NQSW to develop.
6. Gain support from other assessors/supervisors.
7. Address any difficulties you identify early and clearly, and record for evidence.
8. Attend any meetings with colleagues regarding the ASYE.
9. Keep up to date with what's new.
10. Regularly check Skills for Care/BASW/HCPC etc for new information.

DEALING WITH DIFFICULTIES

Though most NQSWs will go through the year with minimal difficulty, you may find that some students will struggle in practice and there will be many reasons for this. Some will find particular aspects of the job hard to manage, for example, being analytical, or they may discover that their personal values pose particular difficulties for them. Whatever the issues, we have to be prepared for and able to address them in a timely and professional manner – with support and encouragement while being honest and open, which can be a tall order at times.

Difficulties should be addressed as you would with any other team member. Address things early even if you feel it is only a small thing. Clarify your concerns and then record them, and draw up a clear action plan with specific targets for improvements and with dates included. Discuss concerns where necessary in your own supervision and share your thoughts there too; use the support you have to help you in this area.

Be honest with the NQSW as soon as you feel there is an issue and ensure that they know that you are offering support and help; this will enable them to have confidence in you and make it easier for them to share their own concerns. Forming an open and trusting relationship from the beginning will ensure that the learning journey is completed as smoothly as possible for both parties.

Case Study – The challenging worker

Have a look at the case study here, which is designed just to get you into thinking about possible issues you may face.

Sue is an NQSW who is newly appointed to Graham's team, having completed her final placement there, where she reportedly did well. Graham was not Sue's practice educator; this was a colleague from another team, who Graham does not have a particularly high opinion of. Graham feels that the ASYE is a real move forward in the social work profession and is looking forward to the challenge of working with Sue during her first year in practice. Graham and Sue have their first supervision session booked for the second week of Sue's employment but before this can happen, Sue comes to Graham and asks for this day off. Graham has already had feedback from team members that Sue has been spending quite a lot of time chatting to her old practice educator and that she has been using the work computer to access her own emails throughout the day.

- o *What are the issues here?*
- o *How should Graham react to the request for the day off?*
- o *What are his priorities in this situation?*
- o *Why might Sue be behaving in this way?*

Can you plan a way forward in this case?

This exercise is designed to challenge and make you think. You could use the PCF and ASYE guidelines and/or the Supervision Standards for guidance and ideas for how you would take things forward. Or, as a supervisor you could discuss this scenario with your manager.

EXERCISES

Whether we are experienced assessors, managers or supervisors, we all get stuck at times and need a bit of help. You may well already have a range of exercises to hand which will aid your assessment but here we offer a few more for your consideration. The following are a series of short exercises which are designed to help you in your work with your NQSW. A number of these exercises can be adapted and used more than once during the year.

Though many of these exercises may provide evidence for assessment and will certainly overlap across the domains, the critical links to the PCF are highlighted below. At the end of each meeting you may want to check with the worker and discuss how they see the session in terms of their development and the PCF and whether they think that these exercises have contributed to their toolkit.

Exercise 1 – Setting the scene
(key links to PCF domains 1, 8)

Designed to be used at the outset of the assessment, the purpose of this exercise is to give you an idea of the NQSW's understanding of the PCF, the Knowledge and Skills statements and also HCPC and their purpose/role.

- How many of the domains of the PCF is the student aware of?

- When did the student first become aware of the PCF and what do they understand the purpose of it is?

- Can they set the PCF in the context of current social work developments?

- How does the PCF relate to not just the ASYE but also CPD and career development?

- Do they know the difference between the PCF, the Knowledge and Skills statements and the HCPC standards?

- Can they give an example of how the PCF and the Knowledge and Skills statements and HCPC standards relate to practice, and where these may overlap or differ?

Exercise 2 – Case discussion
(key links to PCF domains 1, 2, 6, 7, 8)

The purpose of this exercise is to ensure that the NQSW is aware of all issues to consider when reflecting on practice.

Ask the student to reflect upon a piece of practice and to bring written reflection to supervision with them.

- In the session encourage them to think about their reflection and consider the following:
  1. Personal and professional values
  2. Policy and procedure
  3. Legislation and guidance
  4. Ethical practice
  5. Best practice

- Encourage their discussion in a holistic way and get them to really explore the impact of the above on their practice and what they have learned through this process.

- From now on you might refer to this as the 'five-point principle for reflection'.

Exercise 3 – Emotional intelligence and resilience *(key links to PCF domains 1, 3, 6)*

The purpose of this exercise is to encourage the NQSW to consider how their use of self is key to their practice and what impact their own level of emotional intelligence has.

- Supervisor – think about something you have experienced that you are happy to share, that has made you sad, happy or angry.

- Sit back to back with your NQSW.

- Recall one of these experiences and tell the story and say how you were feeling during your experience and why you felt like this.

- Turn back to face one another and ask the NQSW how it felt to hear this story without being able to see your face and see your emotions and how this made the story different.

- Ask the NQSW to consider which feelings were most difficult to empathise with, without seeing your expressions. Which was the easiest to empathise with? Why do they think this is? How did they feel during the time you were telling your story? Why is it important to be able to express our feelings and to understand feelings? Was the experience different when they could not see your face and any hand gestures while you told your story? How could they tell if your feelings were congruent with your words?

- Ask your NQSW to consider the feelings and emotions of service users when they are working with them, for example, when undertaking assessments, and what difference it makes having 'emotional intelligence' and being able to 'tune into' these feelings and how this impacts upon their decision making.

- As the story teller – tell the NQSW how it felt telling your story without being able to see them. Discuss together the importance of communication and how someone else sees and interprets you.

- You may want to take turns with this exercise.

Exercise 4 – Theoretical base
(key links to PCF domains 5, 6)

The purpose of this exercise is to explore with the NQSW their understanding of the relevance of theory to their practice and to embed this into practice.

Ask the NQSW to bring a piece of practice to supervision and to be prepared to discuss it in theoretical terms.

- Ask the NQSW to talk you through the piece of practice in simple terms – don't worry about the theory at this point.

- Did they have a hypothesis beforehand about what might be happening? What did they base this on? Discussion can be around making assumptions here.

- Can they tell you why we need theory and what is the point of it? What would happen if we did not use a theoretical base for our work?

- Can they explain the theories that they feel are relevant and why? What other theories might be relevant?

- Set them a task to find one more relevant theory by the next session.

Exercise 5 – How different am I?
(key links to PCF domains 3, 4, 6)

The purpose of this exercise is to encourage the NQSW to explore the differences that they might have from others within the team and immediate work environment and then with service users, as a way of discovering their own differences and similarities to others, and how this impacts on their practice.

- Encourage the NQSW to describe themselves on different levels – physically, emotionally, culturally and in terms of background and upbringing – ask them just to share as much as they are comfortable with. If you feel you want to, you can do the same but it is not necessary for the purpose of the exercise.

- Ask them to then set themselves within the context of the team or workplace and to think about how different or similar they consider themselves to colleagues. Are there any particular colleagues that they identify with and why is this? What assumptions do they think others may make about them based on the above? Can they give any examples of where this has happened? How did they feel about this? Have they been able to challenge others' preconceived ideas?

- Get the NQSW to consider how their differences or similarities affect their frame of reference and what impact this has on their work in the team.

- Broaden the discussion and encourage them to think about these issues in terms of their work with service users.

Exercise 6 – Making decisions
(key links to PCF domains 1, 6, 7)

The purpose of this exercise is to discuss with the NQSW how they make professional judgements, what factors they consider and how they weigh evidence before coming to a decision.

- Ask the NQSW to think of a decision they have made in their home life which turned out to be the wrong decision. One that required some thought and information gathering – this might be where they went on holiday, where they moved house to, which school a child might attend, a financial decision, etc.

- Ask them how they went about making this decision – what information they needed, how they obtained this, who else might have been involved in this decision, what factors they considered.

- Ask them to describe their analysis and give the rationale for their decision. Get them to defend their decision; are they able to?

- At the end of the exercise ask them which of the factors in this scenario are similar to the ones we might face professionally and what aspects of their decision making would they change in hindsight.

Exercise 7 – Dealing with risk
(key links to PCF domains 2, 7)

The purpose of this exercise is to allow your NQSW to think about the different aspects of risk that they have to manage within their role as a social worker and help them justify these risks. Consider when it is appropriate to take risks and include moral and legal considerations. You can include health and safety risks in your discussion too including safe and lone working.

- Ask your NQSW to think about risk.

- What is a safe risk?

- What risk thresholds are the NQSW used to working with?

- In their own lives, what risks does the NQSW take on a daily basis?

- How do they justify these risks for themselves and their families?

- Is it all right to take a risk if it is justified? How do you know if it is justified?

- What risks do they take unconsciously and how often?

- How and why is it different, taking a risk for service users?

- What risks should service users be able to take and why?

- Discuss with your NQSW what types of risk they think they should be able to manage on their caseloads, on their own, and when they should seek advice.

- Discuss together how you will ensure that you and your NQSW both know when your NQSW is able to increase their level of risk taking.

- Discuss how your NQSW will record and show risks when case recording.

Exercise 8 – Organisational structure (key links to PCF domain 8)

The purpose of this exercise is to find out what the NQSW knows about the structure of your organisation and the roles and responsibilities of senior managers. This exercise may be difficult to do, but it will give an idea of the NQSW's understanding of the organisation, and perhaps you may recognise you need to brush up on your own knowledge too.

- Ask your NQSW to draw an organisational chart from Director or Chief Executive level, etc (depending upon the structure of your organisation) down to their level within the organisational structure.

- Ask them to briefly outline the roles and responsibilities of each post.

- Discuss their understanding of elected members and local councillors and their role within the organisation (if local authority organisation) or funders or commissioners (if third sector).

- Ask your NQSW to discuss their understanding of the organisation's 'Development Plan' and how the plan for the team they are in fits into the overall Plan of the organisation.

- Discuss the importance of strategic planning and the NQSW's awareness of this.

- Ask the NQSW what is their understanding of the service manager, team manager and principal social worker roles (you may have different names for these senior roles).

- Discuss the importance of these structures and how they all impact upon the smooth running of the organisation and service users.

Exercise 9 – Minute taking
(key links to PCF domain 1)

Identify an appropriate meeting you can take your NQSW along to and ask them to minute the meeting for you (even if you don't need minutes). This will give the NQSW an opportunity to improve their active listening skills and record the appropriate concise information. When they have typed up these minutes you can discuss them with the NQSW and identify areas for development. This will allow the NQSW to have a 'safe' learning experience before they have to both chair and minute their own meetings.

Exercise 10 – Values and ethics
(key links to PCF domains 2, 3, 4)

This activity is aimed at getting the NQSW to look at their values and ethics and to consider these in the context of human rights. This will allow them to make some of these difficult discussions within a safe environment. The statements below are bold and are meant to get the student to think carefully about the situations and their decision making. Let the NQSW know that the exercise is not meant to make them feel uncomfortable and they will not be judged on their decisions.

- A 78-year-old woman needs heart medication to keep her alive, which will cost the local health trust £3,000 per week; she has worked and paid tax and national insurance all her working life. A nine-month-old baby needs a life-saving operation which will cost the health trust £100,000 and will then require a long period in special care and ongoing treatment. The baby will still have a life-limiting condition, which is likely to mean they will live only until their teenage years. Who will you support in getting the budget for their needs?

- Three children aged two, four and six have been looked after by the local authority and are to be adopted but finding a family for them all has already taken over a year, without success. At present they are cared for together by the same foster carers. Do you look for separate families for them?

- A 29-year-old man who uses drugs and who has been in rehab a number of times has asked to be recommended for readmission; he says that he has 'found God' and feels that his previous life has been a waste and he wants to move forward positively. There are other people waiting for access to the rehab unit. Do you recommend him?

- The parents of a 20-year-old female with learning difficulties and challenging behaviour have made the decision that they can no longer meet her needs at home and want her to be cared for in a residential home. The only care home that fully meets her needs is 200 miles away and the parents do not drive. How do you proceed?

These statements are thought provoking and aimed at making the NQSW think about their own values and ethics and why they think this way.

Ask the NQSW:

- to discuss each scenario and make their choice with their reasons;
- to consider where their own value base comes from and what experiences they had to make these the foundation of their belief system;
- to discuss the human rights aspects regarding each statement;
- to discuss issues around cost implications for budgets and how this impacts upon decision making;
- to think about advocacy issues for those who cannot speak up for themselves.

Exercise 11 – 'My contribution to the team' (key links to PCF domains 5, 9)

This exercise will help the NQSW to feel that they are part of the team and contributing to the development of the team as a whole and it can be worked on over a period of time, as the worker develops in confidence and competence. The exercise will also give you a valuable opportunity to observe the NQSW working within the team and with others.

Engage a more experienced worker to support you in this exercise and get them to work with the NQSW. Ask the NQSW to choose an interesting case that they have been working on and which they may be finding a particular challenge, and to conduct a piece of relevant research around the issues of the case. Get the NQSW to prepare and present a ten-minute case study to the team, with the support of the senior worker, and to generate a ten-minute debate/discussion around the issues in the case. They should include the social work methodology and theoretical base they have used to inform their practice. Encourage the team to give feedback to the NQSW, especially around any best practice that they identify, and make any suggestions that they may have. Follow this up with a discussion in supervision.

Exercise 12 – 'My professional network' (key links to PCF domain 8)

The purpose of this exercise is to encourage the NQSW to think about the people that inform their practice and the relationships that they need to develop as they progress and to test their knowledge of others' roles and responsibilities.

Ask the NQSW to draw a diagram detailing the professional network that they feel is relevant to their role; this should include all others that they come into contact with on a regular basis. Get them to think about regular and occasional, formal and informal, statutory and non-statutory contacts.

- Ask them to describe each role from their diagram and to tell you about the responsibilities of each person and to talk to you about any issues in practice that they may have when roles conflict.

- Get them to speak about specific cases and relate this to their practice and to talk about both negative and positive experiences they have had with colleagues and why they think that this may be.

- Ask them how they think their network developed and what their plans are to further this in the future.

- What do they think is the most challenging thing about working with others and how can they overcome this?

Exercise 13 – Supervision
(key links to PCF domains 1, 5, 6)

The purpose of this exercise is to help you and your NQSW identify risk/stressors that the NQSW may be dealing with and balance these against the resilience and protective factors in place and make a plan of action to address and monitor this.

We have devised a useful table (Figure 2) that you and your NQSW can use together, in supervision, to help identify and monitor NQSW risks and resilience management. This table helps identify whether your NQSW is at high, medium, low or no risk due to certain risks and stressors that will impact or make a demand upon them within their work. You should consider the resilience factors alongside each risk. This tool should allow you to identify the risk/stressor, record any likely harm and what you can do about this, and then decide when to review this. Figure 3 breaks the process down and gives information for you and your NQSW to consider when using the table. This will help you identify and safeguard against any risks while ensuring you are able to monitor your NQSW against these risks.

Name of Supervisee: Name of Supervisor: Date:

Considerations: (When identifying the factors below you should consider the NQSW's resilience factors)	Level of Risk to worker				Identify likely Harm, Risk or Stressor	Identify Solution	Decision	Review Date
	High	Med	Low	None				
Workload management: Content and type of work; pace of work; physical, environmental, emotional impact of cases on NQSW								
Ability: NQSW's competence level versus demands of the case. Any concerns regarding complexity of case for NQSW?								
Volume: (no of cases): Level of decision making required; time management involved in cases; capacity within team; other cases								
Role: Is worker clear about their role? Ambiguity, role conflict? Are they managing the conflict of organisation versus service user needs?								
Support structures: Does the NQSW have a mentor/co-worker? Do they have support from colleagues? Does the worker feel under pressure?								
Supervision: How often does the NQSW have supervision? Is this too much, or not enough? Type of supervision? Who undertakes the supervision? Is it effective and safe?								
Sickness: Has the NQSW been off sick? How often is this sickness? Is the sickness work related? Is this impacting upon work? Work–life balance?								
Training: Does the worker require additional training? Does training make a difference? Evidence of positive change.								

Supervisee's comments:

Signature:

Supervisor's comments:

Signature:

Figure 2 NQSW risks and resilience management table

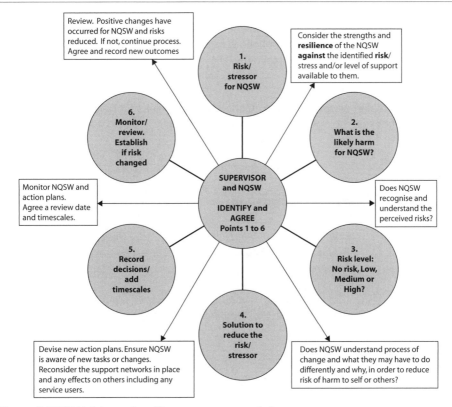

Figure 3 NQSW risks and resilience management diagram

YOUR OWN SUPPORT NETWORK

Remember, too, that you will require support. Even the most experienced of us need this and it is important that this is set up before the year starts. Ensure that you know where to go if you have any issues and make the ASYE a standing item on your own supervision agenda, to ensure that you feel that you have the space to discuss things as the year progresses.

CONCLUSION

This chapter and the exercises within it should be helpful in supporting your NQSW through their first year. As the ASYE continues to develop, you may need to look further afield for support for both NQSWs and assessors. There are already universities offering courses for the NQSW which will help them progress through their ASYE, and some further sources of information are listed below.

We believe that this chapter (and the rest of the book) will give you a range of ideas and encourage you to explore different options in terms of the learning needs for your NQSW. The activities will help you both achieve positive outcomes as you journey together along this exciting year.

Well done for taking on this new task, Good luck and thanks for helping to put *Positive Social Work* back on the agenda for the next generation of professionals.

TAKING IT FURTHER

Hothersall, SJ, Maas-lowit, M (2010) Need, Risk and Protection in Social Work Practice. Exeter: Learning Matters

Taylor, B (2010) Professional Decision Making in Social Work Practice. Exeter: Learning Matters

Websites:

www.basw.co.uk

www.skillsforcare.org.uk

THE TOOLKIT

An electronic version of this Toolkit is available at www.criticalpublishing.com/ asset/126677/1/Positive_Social_Work_Toolkit.pdf

Fill in the Toolkit as you work your way through the chapters. This is your Toolkit and will be different for everyone; it is a live document and represents your journey through your first year in practice (and beyond). We will make suggestions, prompt your thinking with questions, and encourage you to add your own thoughts and to use this to record evidence of developing capability during your ASYE. Try to include specific examples of practice where possible and report outcomes, and get into the habit of completing the document regularly. The Toolkit can be used as a basis for supervision and discussion around progression and links directly to the PCF. To help you in this please also refer to the *Professional Capabilities Framework – Assessed and Supported Year in Employment (ASYE) Level Capabilities* information which can be found on the BASW website. Remember that the Toolkit is a guide; you do not have to use all of the questions here. You may also like to refer back to the chapters in the book to help you and though there are many overlaps, we have identified the ones which are most applicable to the relevant domain within the PCF below. Remember your ASYE is a year-long journey, therefore do not be daunted by this document; it is a tool to help you gather your evidence over the whole year, rather than a 'must do' chore.

Remember – the original College of Social Work, now BASW guidance, states that:

by the end of the ASYE social workers should have consistently demonstrated practice in a wider range of tasks and roles, and have become more effective in their interventions, thus building their own confidence, and earning the confidence of others. They will have more experience and skills in relation to a particular setting and user group, and have demonstrated ability to work effectively on more complex situations. They will seek support in supervision appropriately, whilst starting to exercise initiative and evaluate their own practice.

This is what you are aiming for.

Focus your mind and think about why you became a social worker, what you hope to get out of your chosen profession, what motivates you, why did you choose social work, what are your dreams and aspirations for the future? These are the things that will keep you grounded and that you can reflect upon as you go along. Record your thoughts below:

Remember the evidence is all around you, and you may want to include any of the following in your evidence:

o   Written work – reports, case notes, assessments, reviews/evaluations, case closures, minutes of meetings, supervision notes, team meeting notes, induction record

o   Observations – by your manager/assessor, colleagues

o   Feedback – from colleagues in your own team/agency or others, from service users and carers, from other professionals in other disciplines

o   Training – records, notes, certificates

o   Records of reading – books, websites, journals, articles

o   Visits to other agencies or work shadowing

o   Evidence of regular reflection on your practice

o   Examples from case work, direct work with service users

o   Special projects or specific pieces of work

o   Supervision notes and exercises, preparation records

o   Diary notes and organisation/time management sheets/'to do' lists

o   Reading for specific cases or around particular theory, policy and procedure or legislation

o   Observations of others' practice

o   Joint case working opportunities

o   Please add any others you can think of

PCF 1 – Professionalism

Overview: Your ability to evidence your commitment to the social work profession, and your responsibility and accountability in practice, and your ability to work within regulatory guidelines.

Predominant links to Chapters 2, 3, 4, 6, 7, 8, 9

○ How do you demonstrate that you are able to meet and maintain the HCPC standards? How are you fulfilling the requirements of the Knowledge and Skills statements? Check the standards and think about how you can demonstrate your compliance. Look at each different standard and think of at least one example that you can record. Some questions to ask may include: How have you recognised and responded when vulnerable people have been at risk, how have you worked with service users in a respectful, open and polite manner, how would you define your professional boundaries, which of your own values impact upon your practice and how do you address this, how do you ensure that your practice is inclusive and that this applies to all service users equally, how do you rate your communication skills – written, verbal and non-verbal, when do you work with others from other teams and disciplines and in what contexts, which records do you keep and when – are these kept up to date, which social work theories and models do you use, are these always appropriate, how do you know, which IT systems are you able to use and what impact does this have on your practice, how do you manage confidentiality in difficult circumstances – eg hot desking, mobile working?

○ How do you use supervision? How do you prepare for your meeting, how do you assert your needs, discuss personal and professional issues, reflect on practice, request and accept constructive feedback? How do you include the PCF as a tool to help develop your practice?

○ How are you caring for yourself? How do you ensure a good work–life balance, manage your time effectively, understand and maximise your strengths and identify and manage your own vulnerabilities, and develop your emotional resilience? How do you support the well-being of others?

○ How are you ensuring professional boundaries are in place? How are you sharing your own personal experiences, history and knowledge, setting appropriate ground rules for yourself and your relationships with service users?

○ What personal development goals have you set for yourself – further training courses, shadowing opportunities, supervision discussion, reading, study time?

○ Are you able to challenge colleagues and managers? Can you assert yourself, can you challenge poor practice, and are you able to manage relationships with all colleagues, even though some may be difficult?

Continued overleaf

○ How do you demonstrate your accountability – are your recordings timely and appropriate, can you evidence your decision making, do you accept responsibility for mistakes, are you open to challenge? What are your strategies for managing your time effectively?

○ How are you ensuring that you are presenting yourself as best you can and in the most professional manner – preparation for meetings and observing others chairing, the way you dress, the language you use, your time-keeping and reliability, the relationships you develop with others?

○ How do you contribute to the positive reputation of the profession – how do you interact with colleagues in other teams or services, do you have belief in your convictions, reclaim the professionalism that media often deny, stay positive, motivate and help others believe in social work?

○ Use this space to add your own examples, evidence, plans, reflection.

PCF 2 – Values and Ethics

Overview: How your practice is underpinned by sound professional values and ethics and how you understand and apply the relevant legislation in this area of your work.

Predominant links to Chapters 3, 4, 5, 6, 7, 8, 9

o   How do you ensure that you uphold professional values and ethics – can you identify your own core values, how do your personal and professional values differ, what effect does this have on your work, how does your own personal value base affect the way you work with service users and colleagues, how are you able to reconcile the differences that can exist between professional and service users' values, how do you ensure that you are not imposing your values on others?

o   How do you demonstrate ethical standards in your practice – how do you ensure that ethically sound decisions are made and what is your 'process' for this, how do you manage decisions that challenge your own moral values, how do you include others in this and who might these be, how have you managed ethically difficult situations, can you think of incidents where you have been professionally assertive, what have been the results of this, how did you find this, how have you managed challenge and what part do values and ethics play in this?

o   What part does policy, procedure and legislation play in your seeking to be an ethically sound practitioner, which of these defines your practice, what have you found that has helped or hindered your decision making, in what way?

---

o   Use this space to add your own examples, evidence, plans, reflection.

PCF 3 – Diversity

Overview: Your understanding of how difference shapes the lives of others both individually and collectively and how this can be both positive and negative, and how you are able to effectively challenge when this is required.

Predominant links to Chapters 5, 9

○   Think about the service that you work in and about the diversity of the service user group and think about the cases that you have worked with. How have you actively supported individual or family needs in this area, are there any cases which stand out for any particular reason, can you give examples of where service users have been disadvantaged due to their own personal circumstances, background, attitude or value base, what have you done to support them, how have you encountered oppression and supported individuals to reach their potential, in what ways have you advocated on their behalf?

○   Have you worked with service users who have felt that their circumstances or background have been a positive advantage to them, or that they used their circumstances or background to justify their negative actions or reactions to others or to your intervention, can you think of occasions where you have challenged people in this area, what has been the result? Whether positive or negative, what did you learn from this, how have you helped others to see the oppression and opportunity that can arise from their own experiences?

○   How aware of your own personal and professional power do you feel you are, how does this impact upon your work, can you give both negative and positive examples of this, how do you use your power for the benefit of service users, how does your title and role impact on the development of relationships with others, how do you manage this on a day-to-day basis, how do others' perceptions of you (personally and professionally) and your role affect the manner in which you work?

○   How do you ensure that you challenge and do not collude with people, services or organisations which seek to marginalise others, how do you manage situations where thoughts and opinions are at such odds that no compromise can be found and significant risk or high level of need is apparent?

○   Use this space to add your own examples, evidence, plans, reflection.

PCF 4 – Rights, Justice and Economic Well-being

Overview: The protection of rights and equality and how these principles underline your practice and how you use legislation to support this.

Predominant links to Chapters 4, 5, 9

○ Which legislation, policy and procedures do you use the most in your role in terms of upholding the rights of service users, how does this legislation assist your role and in what ways have you found that you are constrained by this? Which policies and procedures underpin your practice in this area and how do you apply these in your casework? How do these have a direct benefit (or otherwise) on service users, which other services have you used to assist with this and how has this affected the outcome of your work?

○ How do you ensure that the human rights of your service users are upheld? Which rights do you feel are most violated and why, how do you help service users to understand these rights and how do you support their quest for justice and equality?

○ Can you identify the factors in your work with service users which make them vulnerable to oppression, discrimination and poverty? How do you address issues where many of these factors are present and are inter-generational, how has your work helped to address these issues in the short/medium and long term, how do you empower service users to address these factors for themselves, to move forward and to begin to become independent of support services?

○ How have you assisted service users to access your and other services which will support their development and bring about an improvement in their circumstances? Which services have you used to support this, in what ways do you assist service users to gain an independent voice where necessary and enable them to make informed and positive choices in their lives?

○ Use this space to add your own examples, evidence, plans, reflection.

PCF 5 – Knowledge – *link here to the Knowledge and Skills statements*

Overview: The knowledge you have developed in different areas including the law, policy and procedure, human development and the influences upon this. Different social work models and theories, and how you use this knowledge in practice.

Predominant links to Chapters 2, 4, 5, 6, 7, 9

○   Describe your knowledge base. What knowledge do you need to do your job effectively and where does this come from, how have you used the knowledge gained throughout your time at university to your and the service users' best advantage, do you feel that this effectively equipped you for your role, what areas of knowledge do you use daily, weekly or less often, which specialist areas of knowledge do you use in your current role?

○   Which areas of theoretical knowledge do you currently use and how, how have you developed this in practice, what further reading or research have you completed in this area, which areas do you find particularly difficult or challenging, how have you addressed this, are there any theories that you particularly use and apply methodically or habitually, or are there some that you don't – why not? Are you heavily reliant on a few theoretical models, which ones and why? Do you test out different theories, why do you do this?

○   What are the most significant policies and procedures that your practice is guided by, how familiar are you with these, how do they shape your work, do you feel that you understand them all fully?

○   What legislation does your service work under, how does this impact upon your role as a social worker, which pieces of legislation do you use the most, which pose the most challenge, how do you implement the legislation with service users and ensure their understanding and compliance, what action do you take when legal agreements are breached?

○   What social work models do you use when working with service users, are there some that you find work better than others, others that you have yet to try, or some that you find do not work for you – why?

○   What new knowledge have you acquired since you qualified, how did this come about and why, how are you using this in your practice, where has this learning come from, what have you learned from reading, supervision, colleagues, service users or others, what do you feel has been your most valuable lesson and why, how do you keep up to date with new developments in social work, what articles, journals, books or magazine articles have you read?

Continued overleaf

○ Where do you go when you do not know the answer, what happens when you are faced with a situation or question that you do not have an answer for, how do you use others' experience and knowledge to further your own and to benefit the service user, have you identified any gaps in your knowledge in terms of theory, policy and procedure, legislation, what have you done to address this?

○ Use this space to add your own examples, evidence, plans, reflection.

PCF 6 – Critical Reflection and Analysis

Overview: Reflection both in and on practice, using a range of different sources of evidence in order to provide analysis and arrive at sound decisions; and also in order to learn and develop.

Predominant links to Chapters 4, 9

○ What sources of information, evidence and knowledge do you use in your casework, where does this come from, what emphasis do you put on different pieces of information, from different sources, gained in different ways? How do you decide what is important and what is not, what is fact and what is opinion, what is true and untrue, what methods of analysis do you use, how do you decide on the relevance of information, what impact does your subsequent decision making have on service users and the outcome of your work?

○ How effective are your problem-solving skills, how do you decide on a plan of intervention or action, what factors do you weigh when deciding on which option to take? How and when are you able to demonstrate a flexible approach, how do you know when this is appropriate, how creative are you in working with service users, how far are you able to use hypotheses to test out your initial opinions and how does this shape your work and its outcomes?

○ How do you learn best, how do you put previous learning into practice, how do you reflect on what you have learned, how does this help in your professional development, how does what you do now differ from how you would have done things previously, how and why has this come about?

○ How are you using your supervision to reflect upon and analyse your practice, how are you linking intuition and analysis, are you being emotionally intelligible within your practice and decision making?

○ How honest are you able to be with your supervisor and with yourself, can you share your true feelings when things are difficult or you are not coping, are you acknowledging your fears and anxieties?

○ How is your work–life balance, are there any difficulties that are impacting your practice?

○ Use this space to add your own examples, evidence, plans, reflection.

PCF 7 – Intervention and Skills – *link here to the Knowledge and Skills statements*

Overview: How you form positive relationships and how this enables you to balance rights and responsibilities, need and risk and how you use your skills to intervene and improve lives.

Predominant links to Chapters 3, 4, 5, 6, 7, 9

○ How effectively can you communicate with service users, which methods do you use regularly or occasionally, how do you demonstrate that you are a good listener, in what way do you use your body language to communicate with others, how do you ensure that others understand what you are communicating, what methods do you employ to enable service users with special needs to understand your message, how do you ensure that you communicate your message clearly and effectively and check that you have been understood? How do you ensure you gain consent from people with communication or learning difficulties?

○ How do you build relationships with service users, in what ways do you develop a rapport with them, how do you ensure that they are aware of but not disempowered by your role, how do you ensure that service users are clear about your role and its limitations, how open with them are you in this respect?

○ Which methods of social work intervention do you use and why, how do you select your chosen method and how do you know whether it has been effective or not, how do you follow up if things are not going to plan?

○ When do you make written records, how and where, which records have you kept and for what purpose, how do you record disagreements with managers, colleagues and service users and ensure that all views are recorded, how do you demonstrate that you know what is opinion and what is fact, how do you ensure that appropriate access to records is maintained and in line with policy and legislation?

○ How timely and thorough are your assessments? Which theories underpin your work, how do you manage to work with the service user and provide ongoing support at the same time as continuing a period of assessment, how do you structure your work while remaining flexible and being able to respond to ongoing and newly developed need, what is your understanding of the level of risk that your service users may be facing, how do you assess, respond to and manage risk and need in your cases, how have

Continued overleaf

you contributed to plans which ensure the safety and well-being of service users, what strategies have you employed which have reduced the level of risk?

○ Use this space to add your own examples, evidence, plans, reflection.

PCF 8 – Contexts and Organisations

Overview: How you respond to changing situations and circumstances, and how this enables you to work with others while fulfilling your professional responsibilities.

Predominant links to Chapters 2, 3, 4, 5, 6, 7, 8, 9

- How well do you work within your own team, are you a 'team player' or do you prefer to work alone, why? Are there times when you ask for support with your cases and are there times when you have been asked to support others in their work, do you always agree with what is being said or proposed or with action taken either on your own cases or on others, are you confident in offering your professional opinion to more experienced colleagues, do you mind others challenging your views and plans?

- Which other teams do you engage with on a regular basis and in what context, how do you promote multi-agency working, how do you ensure that you have clear roles when working with colleagues from other teams or disciplines, in statutory roles or within the voluntary sector, what do you find the most challenging in this area, have there been any professional disagreements, how have these been resolved, what do you consider the most effective ways in which you have worked together with others, what kinds of communications do you have with other teams and how may this be improved, in what circumstances have you worked to achieve the best outcomes for service users within a multi-agency team, how have you managed the conflict that arises when multi-agency teams have differing roles and agenda and are working under differing legal and policy guidelines?

- Use this space to add your own examples, evidence, plans, reflection.

PCF 9 – Professional Leadership – *Remember to check that this is the most up-to-date version of PCF 9 before beginning your work here, see p 7*

Overview: How you contribute to the profession and to the development of others, and how this enhances the service for all involved.

Predominant links to Chapters 2, 9

○   How do you contribute to the development of others, have you been involved in any special or project work or sat on any working party meetings, have any social work students been placed with the team, how did you support their work, have you been involved in any research, how has this been used to develop your own practice or that of others?

○   Which areas of your work contain an element of teaching? This may be with a service user or a parent/carer or with less experienced colleagues. How has your intervention contributed to them learning or improving existing skills, knowledge or experience, what impact has this had on their development or circumstances?

○   Do you regularly attend and contribute to team or site meetings, have you made any presentations to your team, perhaps sharing your knowledge after you've attended a training course, have you raised issues in meetings which required addressing or which have led to improvements or developments in practice, have you challenged any decisions made in this forum, are you confident in speaking in team meetings, have you chaired or taken the minutes, have you engaged in team case discussions, do you become involved in service evaluation as a part of the team?

○   Use this space to add your own examples, evidence, plans, reflection.

REFERENCES

Acker, GM (1999) The Impact of Clients' Mental Illness on Social Workers' Job Satisfaction and Burnout. *Health and Social Work*, 24: 112–19

Andel, R, Crowe, M, Hahn, EA et al. (2012) Work-Related Stress May Increase the Risk of Vascular Dementia. *Journal of the American Geriatrics Society*, 60(1): 60–7

Bogg, D, Challis, M (2016) *Evidencing CPD: A Guide to Building your Social Work Portfolio*. Northwich: Critical Publishing

Carnall, CA (2007) *Managing Change in Organizations*. London: Prentice Hall International Limited, pp 238–44

Coffey, M, Dudgill, L, Tattersall, A (2004) Research Note: Stress in Social Services Mental Well-being, Constraints and Job Satisfaction. *British Journal of Social Work*, 34(5): 735–46 (cited in Collins, S (2008) Statutory Social Workers, Stress, Job Satisfaction, Coping, Social Support and Individual Differences. *British Journal of Social Work*, 38: 1174)

College of Social Work (September 2012) *PCF20 – Principles for Gathering and Using Feedback from People Who Use Services and Those Who Care for Them*, pp 1–5. Available online at www.basw.co.uk/resources/ tcsw/Assessing%20social%20work%20practice%20against%20the%20PCF.pdf (accessed 8 October 2016)

Collins, S (2007) Social Workers, Resilience, Positive Emotions and Optimism. *Practice: Social Work in Action*, 19(4): 255–69. Available online at www.tandfonline.com/doi/full/10.1080/09503150701728186?src =recsys (accessed 15 October 2016)

Collins, S (2008) Statutory Social Workers: Stress, Job Satisfaction, Coping, Social Support and Individual Differences. *British Journal of Social Work*, 38: 1173–93

Collins, S, Coffey, M, Morris, L (2010) Social Work Students: Stress, Support and Well-Being. *British Journal of Social Work*, 40: 963–82

Collings, J, Murray, P (1996) Predictors of Stress amongst Social Workers: An Empirical Study. *British Journal of Social Work*, 26: 375–87 (cited in Lloyd, C, King, R and Chenoweth, L (2002) Social Work, Stress and Burnout: A Review. *Journal of Mental Health*, 11(3): 255–65)

Department for Education (2015) *Working Together to Safeguard Children: A Guide to Inter-agency Working to Safeguard and Promote the Welfare of Children*. London: Department for Education. Available online at www.gov.uk/government/uploads/system/uploads/attachment_data/file/419595/Working_Together_to_ Safeguard_Children.pdf (accessed 10 October 2016)

Department of Health (2009) *Social Work Task Force Final Report: Building a Safe, Confident Future*. Available online at http://webarchive.nationalarchives.gov.uk/20130401151715/https:/www.education.gov. uk/publications/eOrderingDownload/01114-2009DOM-EN.pdf (accessed 30 September 2016), pp 17–18.

Dunham, J (1988) Review of the Stress Research Literature in Three Helping Occupations (cited in Thompson, N, Murphy, M, Stadling, S (1994) *Dealing With Stress*. Basingstoke: Palgrave Macmillan)

Eborall, C, Garmeson, K (2001) Desk Research on Recruitment and Retention in Social Care and Social Work, London: Business and Industrial Market of Research (cited in Collins, S (2007) Social Workers, Resilience, Positive Emotions and Optimism. *Practice: Social Work in Action*, 19(4): 255–69)

Egan, M (1993) Resilience at the Front Lines: Hospital Social Work with AIDS Patients and Burnout. *Social Work in Health Care*, 18: 109–25

Evans, C (2008) *Time Management for Dummies* (UK Edition). Chichester: John Wiley & Sons

Festinger, L (1957) *A Theory of Cognitive Dissonance*. California: Stanford University Press

Field, P, Jasper, C, Littler, L (2016) *Practice Education in Social Work: Achieving Professional Standards*. Northwich: Critical Publishing

Forster, M (2006) *Do It Tomorrow and Other Secrets of Time Management*. London: Hodder & Stoughton

General Social Care Council (GSCC) (2005) *Post Qualifying Framework for Social Work Education and Training*. London: GSCC

Goleman, D (1995) *Emotional Intelligence*. New York: Bantam Books

Grimes, R (2005) cited in http://nation.uk.com/imgs/pdfs/CopingWithChange.pdf (accessed 7 July 2012)

Hackett, J, Tebow, D (2012) *Emotional Intelligence: Complete Guide To Improving Your Emotional Intelligence. Five Skills of Improving Emotional Intelligence the Right Way*. Blue Shift Publishing LLC, Kindle Edition

HCPC (2016) *The Standards of Conduct, Performance and Ethics*. London: HCPC. Available online at www.hcpc-uk.org/ (accessed 24 September 2016)

Health & Safety Executive (HSE) (2009) *How To Tackle Work-Related Stress. A Guide for Employers on Making the Management Standards Work*. London: HSE

Health & Safety Executive (HSE) (2011) *Stress and Psychological Disorders*. London: HSE, pp 1–6

Health & Safety Executive's Labour Force Survey (LFS) 2014/15. Available online at www.hse.gov.uk/Statistics/causdis/stress/index.htm (accessed 27 September 2016)

Hersey, P, Blanchard, KH (1988) *Management of Organizational Behaviour: Utilizing Human Resources*. Upper Saddle River, NJ: Prentice Hall (cited in Huczynski, A, Buchanan, D (2001) *Organizational Behaviour: An Introductory Text*, 4th edn. Harlow: Pearson Education, pp 722–4)

Hogarth, T, Hasluck, C, Pierre, G (2001) *Work-Life Balance 2000: Results from the Baseline Study of Work-Life Balance*. London: Department for Education and Employment. Available online at http://dera.ioe.ac.uk/4596/1/RR249.PDF (accessed 17 October 2016)

Hooker, H, Neathey, F, Casebourne, J, Munro, M (2011) *The Third Work-Life Balance Employee Survey: Main Findings* (Revised edition with corrected figures). London: Department for Business Innovation and Skills. Available online at www.gov.uk/government/uploads/system/uploads/attachment_data/file/32187/07-714x-third-work-life-balance-employee-survey-findings-revised.pdf (accessed 4 October 2016)

Hothersall, SJ, Maas-Lowit M (2010) *Need, Risk and Protection in Social Work Practice*. Exeter: Learning Matters

Howe, D (2008) *The Emotionally Intelligent Social Worker*. Basingstoke: Palgrave Macmillan

HSE (2016) Work Related Stress, Anxiety and Depression Statistics in Great Britain 2016. Available online at www.hse.gov.uk/Statistics/causdis/stress/stress.pdf?pdf=stress (accessed 7 January 2017)

Huxley, PS, Evans, C, Gately, M, Webber, A, Mears, S, Pajak, T, Kendall, J, Medina, J, Katona, C (2005) Stress and Pressure in Mental Health Social Work: The Worker Speaks. *British Journal of Social Work*, 35(7): 1063–79 (cited in Collins, S (2007) Social Workers, Resilience, Positive Emotions and Optimism. *Practice: Social Work in Action*, 19(4): 255–69)

Judd, RG, Johnston, LB (2012) Ethical Consequences of Using Social Network Sites for Students in Professional Social Work Programs. *Journal of Social Work Values and Ethics*, 9(1): 5–12

Kinman, G, Grant, L (2011) Exploring Stress Resilience in Trainee Social Workers: The Role of Emotional and Social Competencies. *British Journal of Social Work*, 41: 261–75

Kolb, DA (1984) *Experiential Learning: Experience as the Source of Learning and Development*. Englewood Cliffs, NJ: Prentice Hall

Koprowska, J (2014) *Communication and Interpersonal Skills in Social Work*. Exeter: Learning Matters

Laming, H (2009) *The Protection of Children in England: A Progress Report*. London: DOH Crown. Available online at www.education.gov.uk/publications/eOrderingDownload/HC-330.pdf (accessed 5 October 2012)

Lewin, K (1947) Frontiers in Group Dynamics: Concept Method and Reality in Social Science; Social Equilibria and Social Change. *Human Relations*, 1: 5–41

Lloyd, C, King, R, Chenoweth, L (2002) Social Work, Stress and Burnout: A Review. *Journal of Mental Health*, 11(3): 255–65

Lomax, R, Jones, K, Leigh, S, Gay, C (2010) *Surviving Your Social Work Placement*. Basingstoke: Palgrave Macmillan

Martin, V, Charlesworth, J, Henderson, E (2010) *Managing in Health and Social Care*, 2nd edn. London: Routledge

Maslach, C, Jackson, S, Leiter, M (1996) *Maslach Burnout Inventory Manual*. Palo Alto: Consulting Psychologists Press (cited in Lloyd, C, King, R and Chenoweth, L (2002) Social Work, Stress and Burnout: A Review. *Journal of Mental Health*, 11(3): 255–65)

Masson, H, Morrison, T (1991) A 24 Hour Duty System: Using Practitioner Research to Manage the Stress. *British Journal of Social Work,* 21 (cited in Thompson, N, Murphy, M, Stadling, S (1994) *Dealing With Stress*. Basingstoke: Palgrave Macmillan)

Matzke, D (2012) *Emotional Intelligence in a Nutshell – Personality Patterns for Personal Effectiveness*. CreateSpace, Kindle Edition.

Mayer, JD, Salovey, P (1997). What is Emotional Intelligence? In Salovey, P, Sluyter, DJ (eds), *Emotional Development and Emotional Intelligence: Educational Implications*. New York, NY: Basic Books, pp 3–31.

Maylor, H (2005) *Project Management*, 3rd edn. Harlow: Pearson Education Limited

McLeod, SA (2008) *Simply Psychology; Cognitive Dissonance*. Available online at www.simplypsychology. org/cognitive-dissonance.html (accessed 16 October 2016)

Mindtools.com (2012) *How Good Is Your Time Management?* Available online at www.mindtools.com/pages/article/newHTE_88.htm (accessed 10 September 2016)

Moon, J (2004) *A Handbook of Reflective and Experiential Learning Theory and Practice*. Abingdon: RoutledgeFalmer

Morrison, T (2005) *Staff Supervision in Social Care*, 3rd edn. Hove, Brighton: Pavilion Publishing and Media Ltd

Morrison, T (2007) Emotional Intelligence, Emotion and Social Work: Context, Characteristics, Complications and Contribution. *British Journal of Social Work*, 37(2): 245–63. Available online at http://bjsw.oxfordjournals.org/content/37/2/245.full.pdf+html (accessed 17 October 2017)

Morrison, T, Wonnacott, J (2010) *Supervision: Now or Never. Reclaiming Reflective Supervision in Social Work*. Available online at www.local.gov.uk/c/document_library/get_file?uuid=545d7e64-f5b1-43a0-b4cb-46a03c7acce6&groupId=10180 (accessed 15 October 2016)

Munro, E (2011a) *The Munro Review of Child Protection: Final Report – A Child-Centred System*. London: Department for Education. Available online at www.gov.uk/government/uploads/system/uploads/attachment_data/file/175391/Munro-Review.pdf (accessed 17 October 2016)

Munro, E (2011b) *The Munro Review of Child Protection – Interim Report: The Child's Journey*. London: Department for Education. Available online at www.gov.uk/government/uploads/system/uploads/attachment_data/file/206993/DFE-00010-2011.pdf (accessed 17 October 2016)

Munro, E (2011c) *Young Persons' Guide to the Munro Review of Child Protection*. Department for Education. Available online at www.gov.uk/government/publications/young-persons-guide-to-the-munro-review-of-child-protection (accessed 17 October 2016)

Oko, J (2011) *Understanding and Using Theory in Social Work*. Exeter: Learning Matters

Palfreyman, P (2010) *Stress at Work Policy*. Peterborough: NHS. Available online at www.peterborough.nhs.uk/documents/Freedom%20of%20Information/Policies_and_procedures/Risk_Policies_N__Z/Stress_at_Work_Policy_-_February_2010.pdf?preventCache=08%2F04%2F2010+08%3A43 (accessed 19 January 2013)

Payne, WL (1983/1986). A Study of Emotion: Developing Emotional Intelligence; Self Integration; Relating to Fear, Pain and Desire. Dissertation Abstracts International, 47, p. 203A (University microfilms No. AAC 8605928)

Rose, M (2003) Good Deal, Bad Deal? Job Satisfaction in Occupations. *Work, Employment & Society*, 17(3): 503–30 (cited in Collins, S (2007) Social Workers, Resilience, Positive Emotions and Optimism. *Practice:*

Social Work in Action, 19(4): 255–69 and Collins, S (2008) Statutory Social Workers: Stress, Job Satisfaction, Coping, Social Support and Individual Differences. *British Journal of Social Work*, 38: 1173–93)

Rush, G (2009) *Post Qualifying Child Care Social Work: Developing Reflective Practice*. London: Sage

Salovey, P, Mayer, JD (1990) Emotional Intelligence. *Imagination, Cognition, and Personality*, 9: 185–211

Seibert, KW, Daudelin, MW (1999) *The Role of Reflection in Managerial Learning Theory*. Westport: Research and Practice Quorum Books

Senge, P (1990) *The Fifth Discipline: The Art and Practice of the Learning Organization*, 1st edn. London: Doubleday

Senge P (2006) *The Fifth Discipline: The Art and Practice of the Learning Organization*, 2nd edn. London: Doubleday

Sidell, N, Smiley, D (2008) *Professional Communication Skills in Social Work*. Boston: Allyn & Bacon/ Longman

Skills for Care, CWDC (2007) *Providing Effective Supervision. A Workforce Development Tool, Including a Unit of Competence and Supporting Guidance*. Leeds: Skills for Care and CWDC

Somerset Partnership NHS (2016) *Clinical Supervision Policy*. NHS Foundation Trust: Somerset Partnership. Available online at www.sompar.nhs.uk/media/2900/clinical-supervision-policy-v6mar-2016. pdf (accessed 16 October 2016)

Stephen, W, Cooper, L (2002) *Managing Workplace Stress. A Best Practice Blueprint*. Chichester: John Wiley & Sons Ltd

Stevens, J, Brown, J, Lee, C (2004) *The Second Work-Life Balance Study: Results from the Employees' Survey*. London: MORI.

Stranks, J (2005) *Stress at Work: Management and Prevention*. Oxford: Elsevier Butterworth-Heinemann

Sutherland, VJ, Cooper, GL (2000) *Strategic Stress Management. An Organisational Approach*. Basingstoke: Palgrave

Taylor, B (2010) *Professional Decision Making in Social Work Practice (Post Qualifying Social Work Practice)*. Exeter: Learning Matters

The Open University (2007) *T889 Problem Solving and Improvement: Quality and Other Approaches; Block 3 Techniques*. Waldon Hall, Milton Keynes: The Open University, p 141

Thompson, N, Murphy, M, Stadling, S (1994) *Dealing With Stress*. Basingstoke: The Macmillan Press Ltd

Thorndike, EL (1920). Intelligence and Its Uses. *Harper's Magazine*, 140: 227–35 . Available online at www.socialsuccess.info/review_thorndike_intelligence_and_its_uses.html (accessed 10 October 2016)

Tovey, W (2007) *The Post-Qualifying Handbook for Social Workers*. London: Jessica Kingsley Publishers

Um, MY, Harrison, DF (1998) Role Stressors, Burnout, Mediators, and Job Satisfaction: A Stress-Strain-Outcome Model and an Empirical Test. *Social Work Research*, 22: 100–15 (cited in Lloyd, C, King, R and Chenoweth, L (2002) Social Work, Stress and Burnout: A Review. *Journal of Mental Health* 11(3): 255–65)

Wonnacott, J (2012) *Mastering Social Work Supervision*. London: Jessica Kingsley

Williams, S, Cooper, L (2002) *Managing Workplace Stress: A Best Practice Blueprint*. Chichester: John Wiley & Sons

www.helpguide.org/mental/work_stress_management.htm (accessed 30 September 2016)

www.hse.gov.uk/stress/research.htm (accessed 4 June 2016)

www.hse.gov.uk/pubns/indg430.pdf (accessed 10 October 2016)

www.hse.gov.uk/stress/standards/step1/index.htm (accessed 14 August 2016)

www.nhs.uk/Conditions/stress-anxiety-depression/Pages/understanding-stress.aspx (accessed 6 January 2017)

www.scribd.com/doc/19444567/Individual-Learning (accessed 15 October 2016)

INDEX